Creating the High Schools of Our Choice

Tim Westerberg, Ph.D.

EYE ON EDUCATION
6 Depot Way West, Suite 106
Larchmont, N.Y. 10538

Library of Congress Cataloging-in-Publication Data

Westerberg, Tim.
  Creating the high schools of our choice : a principal's perspective on making high school reform a reality / Tim Westerberg.
      p. cm.
  Includes bibliographical references and index.
  ISBN 1-59667-040-1 (alk. paper)
  1. School principals—United States. 2. School management and organization—United States. 3. Education, Secondary—United States. 4. Educational change—United States. I. Title.
  LB2831.92.W48 2007
  373.12'012—dc22

                          2006102578

Production services:
UB Communications
10 Lodge Lane
Parsippany, NJ 07054
973.331.9391

Also available from Eye On Education

What Great Principals Do *Differently*:
15 Things That Matter Most
Todd Whitaker

What Successful Principals Do!
169 Tips for Principals
Franzy Fleck

Improving Your School One Week At a Time:
Building the Foundation for Professional Teaching & Learning
Jeffrey Zoul

Lead With Me:
A Principal's Guide to Teacher Leadership
Gayle Moller and Anita Pankake

The Instructional Leader's Guide to
Informal Classroom Observations
Sally J. Zepeda

Lead Me—I Dare You!
Sherrel Bergman and Judith Brough

Countdown to the Principalship:
A Resource Guide for Beginning Principals
O'Rourke, Provenzano, Bellamy, and Ballek

Smart, Fast, Efficient:
The New Principals' Guide to Success
Leanna Stohr Isaacson

BRAVO Principal!
Sandra Harris

The Administrator's Guide to
School Community Relations, Second Edition
George E. Pawlas

School Leader Internship: Developing, Monitoring,
and Evaluating Your Leadership Experience, 2nd Ed.
Martin, Wright, Danzig, Flanary, and Brown

Talk It Out!
The Educator's Guide to Successful Difficult Conversations
Barbara E. Sanderson

Making the Right Decisions:
A Guide for School Leaders
Douglas J. Fiore and Chip Joseph

Dealing with Difficult Teachers, Second Edition
Todd Whitaker

Dealing with Difficult Parents
(And with Parents in Difficult Situations)
Todd Whitaker and Douglas Fiore

20 Strategies for
Collaborative School Leaders
Jane Clark Lindle

Great Quotes for Great Educators
Todd Whitaker and Dale Lumpa

Elevating Student Voice:
How To Enhance Participation, Citizenship, & Leadership
Nelson Beaudoin

Stepping Outside Your Comfort Zone:
Lessons for School Leaders
Nelson Beaudoin

What Great Teachers Do *Differently*:
14 Things That Matter Most
Todd Whitaker

Motivating & Inspiring Teachers
The Educational Leader's Guide for Building Staff Morale
Todd Whitaker, Beth Whitaker, and Dale Lumpa

The Principal as Instructional Leader:
A Handbook for Supervisors
Sally J. Zepeda

Instructional Leadership for School Improvement
Sally J. Zepeda

Data Analysis for Continuous School Improvement
Victoria L. Bernhardt

To my wife, Gayle,
and our children,
Wendy, Brian, Rachel, McCabe, and Mackenzie,
whose never-failing support,
encouragement, and demand for financial resources
keep me happy and productive.

Foreword

Tim Westerberg's book *Creating the High School of Our Choice: A Principal's Perspective on Making High School Reform a Reality* provides readers with an "inside the lines" view and approach to high school reform. Littleton High School is one of three high schools detailed in NASSP's 2004 publication *Breaking Ranks II: Strategies for Leading High School Reform*.

High school reform is high on the agenda of national, state, and local leaders. The pressure on high school principals to redesign their schools by raising expectations, increase the rigor of instruction, open access to advanced placement courses, decrease the number of drop-outs, increase post-secondary readiness, and make Adequate Yearly Progress (AYP), as required in the No Child Left Behind legislation, drives the focus of principals throughout the nation.

The plethora of "how to" guides on reforming high schools presents those interested in reforming their schools with the dilemma of choosing which of the many market resources will best support their redesign efforts. This book builds on the successful recommendations and strategies embodied in NASSP's major reform guide, *Breaking Ranks II*, by capturing the implementation of successful reforms at Littleton High School. There is an old adage that states, "A person with an argument is never at the mercy of a person with experience." Tim Westerberg's experience is evident on every page of this book.

NASSP's 2006 National High School Principal of the Year, Dr. Mel Riddile often says, "Best practices don't travel well." It isn't a simple process to take others' successes and automatically implement those practices without adaptation. This book offers the reader detailed how to information that allows for adaptation of best practices in leadership, personalization, curriculum, instruction, and assessment. Dr Westerberg's insights about the successes and challenges in establishing a vision and creating a culture of openness to new ideas are apparent throughout the book. Each chapter contains specific and detailed information, including copies of the principal's newsletter, faculty meeting agenda, curricula design rubrics, and other tools that assist in an overall reform effort.

I encourage every high school principal to place this book along side *Breaking Ranks II* on his or her desk to serve as a guide to the journey through planning and implementing the redesign of the high school that he or she leads.

Gerald N. Tirozzi
Executive Director, NASSP

Table of Contents

Introduction

Creating the Future

It seems that now, more than at any time during my 26 years as a high school principal, principals and other school leaders are talking about losing control over their own professional destinies, their schools, and even their day-to-day lives. *No Child Left Behind* is the latest "villain," with mandated state testing that largely dictates curricula, "highly-qualified" criteria for hiring teachers and instructional paraprofessionals, and threats of sanctions if schools do not meet adequate yearly progress (AYP) goals. Jamie Volmer (2004), an Iowa businessman turned motivational speaker, has expressed his bewilderment over the contradiction between how parents feel about their local schools and the pressure schools are under to change with the question, "How can you satisfy your customers but at the same time be at risk?" The concept of local control seems to be losing its appeal with the general population, including in my home state of Colorado where a constitutional guarantee of local control over education seems to be ignored in favor of shifting more and more decisions about education to the state level. Add to that the many state and federal regulations regarding safety, community participation in school decision making, fiscal responsibility, equal opportunity guarantees, and accountability for results, and a beleaguered high school principal can feel that if she is creating the future at all, it isn't the future of her choice.

The greater involvement of state and federal policy makers in education in this country is reality. The *No Child Left Behind* act represents the greatest intrusion by the federal government into education in the history of this country. That does not, however, diminish the responsibility that high school principals have for leading their communities in creating better schools for kids. In fact, it heightens that responsibility. At a recent high school summit in Colorado, Tom Vander Ark of the Bill and Melinda Gates Foundation said, "You [high school principals] can do more to change the way a community thinks about itself, its children, and its future than any other person in the community, state, or nation." (CASE High School Summit, Copper Mountain, Colorado, 10 June 2004.) The fact of the matter is that of the thousands of decisions made every week affecting children in schools, a great number, and the most important, of those decisions are made by those who work with students on a daily basis—teachers and principals. That is why the title of my monthly newsletter and my motto for the twenty-six years that I was in the captain's chair was "Creating the Future of Our Choice." In the words of Max DePree, ". . . the future can be created, not simply experienced or endured" (1997, p. 22).

That is also the message of this book. The current call for principal leadership in America's high schools is further testimony that principals play key roles in creating schools where kids learn, schools where kids and teachers want to be, schools in which both teachers and students are open to new ideas—in short, the kinds of schools we want.

A Call to Action

Nowhere is the call for principal leadership in creating the high schools of our choice made more clear and compelling than in The National Association of Secondary School Principals' seminal work, *Breaking Ranks II: Strategies for Leading High School Reform* (NASSP, 2006). I had the privilege of joining Ted Sizer on stage at NASSP's 2004 national convention for the release of that publication, and the school in which I served as principal for twenty years, Littleton High School (Colorado), was one of three high schools profiled in the book. In fact, my involvement with NASSP's *Breaking Ranks* series goes back much further than that. From 1994–1996, I was a member of the NASSP/Carnegie commission that wrote *Breaking Ranks: Changing an American Institution* (NASSP, 1996); from 1996–1999, I served on NASSP's Breaking Ranks Advisory Committee. Through these experiences, I became quite familiar with the contents of both *Breaking Ranks* and *Breaking Ranks II*, as well as with the implementation challenges that accompany them.

The original *Breaking Ranks* document served as a manifesto for high school reform—a statement of principles by practitioners (principals) addressed in part to teachers and administrators, but also to policy makers. One finds among its 82 recommendations, for example, belief statements about curriculum, instruction, and school environments, as well as about external alliances, union contracts, and district- and state-provided resources. *Breaking Ranks II*, on the other hand, is written as a field guide for principals with an emphasis on implementation strategies. It reduces the number of recommendations from 82 to 31, with those 31 recommendations clustered under three headings—Collaborative Leadership; Personalization; and Curriculum, Instruction, and Assessment. In commissioning *Breaking Ranks II*, NASSP was responding to feedback from the field that indicated that practitioners in general and principals in particular needed something more "user friendly" to guide their school-transformation efforts.

This author believes that the books and other resources of the *Breaking Ranks* series form an excellent foundation upon which to build a high school transformation effort. But I also know that personal accounts of others going through similar experiences—in this case, high school principals leading high school reform efforts based on *Breaking Ranks* recommendations—are critical to turning a vision into a concrete image. It is through the experiences of others that we begin to see the possibilities in our own situation.

Creating the High Schools of Our Choice represents the combination of over thirty years of experiences, research, anecdotes, and thinking about high schools, the purposes they serve in a democratic society, and the aspirations, motivations, and needs of the people who work and learn in them. It is intended to be both thought-provoking and a "how to" book, and it is written for principals and other members of leadership teams who want to take their schools to the next level of thinking and acting, whatever that level might be. To be sure, schools differ with regard to demographics, resources, challenges, capacity, and readiness for change. But the lessons here have value for all high schools, translated where needed to fit the context of the local school community.

Creating the High Schools of Our Choice has a structure that parallels that of *Breaking Ranks II:* that is, its seven chapters are tied to the BR II headings Collaborative Leadership; Personalization; and Curriculum, Instruction, and Assessment. What you will get from reading this book are philosophical and research-based underpinnings, specific strategies, concrete examples, and leadership recommendations for each of the three major categories of school reform identified in *Breaking Ranks II*. What you do with what you get has endless possibilities for making your school a better place for kids and for teachers.

This is a book about possibilities—the possibilities created by acting upon the beliefs that high school principals can control their own professional destinies and that high school principals can and must lead their school communities in creating the high schools of our choice. As futurist Gary Marx reminds us, in this fast-changing world every institution, including education, will have to be renewed: "Either we can take the lead to engage people in that renewal, or others will do it for us . . . . We have a choice. We can either defend what we have . . . or create what we need" (2006, pp. 34 and 1).

In the words of Sitting Bull, "Let us put our minds together and see what kind of life we can make for our children."

Part I

Collaborative Leadership, Professional Learning Communities, and the Strategic Use of Data

Chapter 1

Creating High Schools Where Teachers Want to Be

Studs Terkel (1972) in his book *Working* has this to say about the importance of meaningful work to human beings: "It [the book] is about a search, too, for daily meaning as well as daily bread, for recognition as well as cash, for astonishment rather than torpor; in short, for a sort of life rather than a Monday through Friday sort of dying. Perhaps immortality, too, is part of the quest" (p. xi).

A quote from one of the workers Terkel interviewed for his book clearly and concisely summarizes what we are all looking for in our work: "I think most of us are looking for a calling, not a job" (p. xxiv).

Astonishment rather than torpor. A calling, not a job. I have been in too many schools where teachers seem to be simply putting in their time. There is little joy or excitement in faculty meetings, in the faculty lounge, or in faculty office areas. There is little interaction, at least on any substantive level, among members of the faculty and staff. Teachers, young and old, are counting off the days until the end of the year, or perhaps even until the end of their careers. People come to work, do their jobs, and function in relative isolation. Too many schools, in short, do not provide the kind of work environment that causes teachers to want to be there. Little wonder that we lose fifty percent of teachers from the profession after five years, which is a tragic waste of human potential and financial resources. Furthermore, we can predict the effect on students' eagerness to be at school if teachers are projecting an attitude that lacks enthusiasm for the workplace. As Seymour Sarason (1990) noted, "It is virtually impossible to create and sustain over time conditions for productive learning for students when they do not exist for teachers" (p. 45). And according to futurist Gary Marx (2006), "Generational experts remark that the opportunity to learn new things and build skills will be like a magnet for recruiting

3

and keeping talented people who were just moving into education careers at the turn of the 21st century" (p. 42).

We spend too much of our lives at work for the workplace not to be an intellectually stimulating and socially enjoyable environment. Workplaces, and particularly schools, ought to be places where we are challenged to think deeply about important issues and where we enjoy the company of our colleagues. Schools ought to be places where laughter is heard frequently, places in which the people who work and learn there are having fun.

Breaking Ranks II (2004) includes nine recommendations that have to do with creating the kind of culture that nurtures growth on the part of everyone in the school community, recommendations that range from leadership to partnership and from collaboration to community. What might these recommendations look like in practice? What possibilities await reform-minded school leaders here?

Schools As Intellectually Stimulating Places in Which to Work

Our early school restructuring years in the late 1980s and early 1990s (the Direction 2000 years) taught us what it was like to work in an environment saturated with stimulating and creative ideas, controversy, a compelling vision for the future, and common goals and objectives. Littleton High School has been striving, sometimes struggling, to maintain that environment ever since.

In *Leadership on the Line: Staying Alive through the Dangers of Leading*, Ronald A. Heifetz and Marty Linsky (2002) propose that "leadership requires disturbing people—but at a rate they can absorb" (p. 20). Over the years I have taken great pride in "disturbing" people at Littleton High School and in the Littleton High School community, and they have responded by taking great joy in disturbing me and one another. Creative dissonance makes for an intellectually stimulating environment in a school. There are a couple of strategies that I have found particularly useful in stimulating thinking and debate—challenging members of the school community with what I think and challenging members of the faculty with what other people think.

The title of my monthly newsletter article to the Littleton High School faculty and community was "Creating the Future of Our Choice." Each month I tried to do more than just report on what was going on at Littleton High School. Instead, or perhaps in addition to that, I tried to provoke thought and discussion on an important subject facing either Littleton High School or high school education in general. Topics over the years included performance-based graduation requirements, schoolwide power standards, grading practices, standards-based math curricula, constructivism as a guiding learning theory, student advisement programs, at-risk intervention, diversity, the role of technology, and the impact of state testing on school programs and priorities (see Figure 1). Those articles sometimes prepared the way in our community, particularly with parents, for initiatives about to get underway at our school and often generated reactions from parents, students, or faculty.

In my early days at Littleton High School, my newsletter article was entitled "What If...?" That title served a similar purpose in that it was intended to get faculty and other members of the school community thinking about why we do the things we do and what might happen for kids if we were to do some of those things differently. The "What If...?" series played a major role in launching our school transformation initiative of the late 1980s, "Direction 2000."

How many faculty members or parents really want to read an article month after month that seldom goes beyond reporting on the predictable and sanitized day-to-day activities of the school? Newsletter articles should be used to start people in the school community thinking and talking about important educational issues facing the school. Newsletters are a way of "disturbing people at a rate they can absorb."

Figure 1

NEWSLETTER: CREATING THE FUTURE...

Tim Westerberg

Principal

Two years ago I wrote the following position paper in response to those in the community who expressed a desire to know how Littleton High School would accommodate new legislation mandating annual state testing and School Accountability Reports (school report cards). This fall our School Accountability Committee included that same paper as part of our School Improvement Plan and asked that it be distributed to our parent community. The paper is printed here in serve of that request.

The administration and faculty at Littleton High School value high student performance on state academic content standards as measured by the Colorado Student Assessment Program (CSAP) as well as preparedness for higher education as measured by the ACT, and we intend to remain fully accredited by the Colorado Department of Education. However, these goals are only two of several of importance to us and to our community. Therefore, the amount of attention these goals receive and the resources allocated to them are necessarily limited.

Expectations of accountability, the realities of open enrollment, and our need to continue to garner support and trust from the community more than suggest that it is in the school's best interest for our students to perform well on CSAP and ACT tests. Both tests play a major

role in determining our accreditation status. Failure to perform competitively in these areas will make it difficult for us to maintain our financial and enrollment base and to focus on the full spectrum of outcomes that have made Littleton High School a premier school in the Denver area for 100 years. But therein lies the difficulty. Our plate is already pretty full.

What are some of these other valued outcomes that Littleton High School is not willing to sacrifice on the altars of CSAP and ACT? Experience tells us that Littleton parents care a great deal, for example, about a variety of performance indicators tied to the college admissions process. What would happen if Littleton High School was fully accredited based on CSAP and ACT scores but experienced a decline in SAT, Advanced Placement (AP), and international Baccalaureate (IB) scores, as well as in college admissions rate? Not a pretty picture. In fact, preparing students for life directly after high school, be it higher education or work, is a very important goal in this community. We cannot afford to divert much attention or many resources away from these goals.

How about the arts? Should human and financial resources devoted to these programs be reduced to better prepare for the CSAP and ACT tests? Again, community values suggest not. The same can be said about athletics, and programs and people that help ensure a

safe and caring environment at Littleton High School.

Finally, there is the issue of the kind of education the Littleton High School faculty and administration is dedicated to delivery. Of course we want our students to know things, the kinds of things represented by state content standards. But our notion of what it means to be well educated goes well beyond that. The Littleton High School vision statement perhaps says it best.

"America needs young people who know how to learn as well as how to read, write, speak, and compute. America needs young people with strong interpersonal skills, the ability to contribute to economic productivity and social progress and justice. America needs young people who can acquire, analyze, and apply information, so as to think creatively, and solve problems.

As workers, parents, citizens, and individuals, members of the next generation should know how to question, invent, anticipate and dream.

We of the Littleton High School community should work every day to help young people do these things, so that they can move, at last, beyond us, each prepared to make a living, make a life and make a difference."

How will we respond to state testing and the annual School Accountability Report? Well, we'll do what we've always done. We'll do our best without losing sight of our goals.

In a keynote address, Bertice Berry (2004) said it well: "Inbreeding does not give birth to genius." Another way to challenge thinking and to create an environment that is intellectually stimulating is to expose teachers to articles written by leading thinkers in our field on subjects of importance to high school education. One of the standing jokes around Littleton High School has to do with the number of articles I copied and placed in teachers' mailboxes. I know that not everyone read every article. Teachers are busy people, and each topic appeals to some people and not to others. But every article was read by at least some people, and most articles stimulated some kind of response from someone on the faculty. Provocative newsletter articles and professional readings help to make high schools places where teachers want to be.

The Importance of Humor

As has already been mentioned, high schools where teachers (and students) want to be are high schools in which people are having fun. Laughter is important in almost every situation, including informal interactions and more formal faculty meetings. Story telling, and particularly humorous story telling, is welcome. Practical jokes should be encouraged.

Every school should have people in charge of humor and practical jokes. Littleton High School certainly has leaders in this regard, and for the purposes of this publication, we will call them Marcia and Erna. Marcia can be counted on each fall to forge the signature of the school principal onto a letter demanding that new teachers schedule an appointment with the principal to go over lesson plans for the first few weeks of school. Each year I forget about that prank until I see the line of new teachers at my secretary's desk scheduling appointments.

Erna can be counted on throughout the year to send notes to individual members of the staff, allegedly from some other member of the staff, asking for pointed information on a sensitive topic or, perhaps, suggesting amorous intents. Someone is always "stealing" faculty pictures out of mailboxes when they come in each fall for nefarious purposes sprung on unsuspecting staff members after the original "theft" has long been forgotten. Most years, someone on the staff gets a phone message in his or her mailbox asking for a returned call to Myra Mains at a number which, unbeknownst to that staff member, is the number for a local funeral home.

Storytelling is very important to preserving important aspects of a school's culture. At a faculty retreat in October of 2004, Marcia and Erna, along with another of their veteran teaching buddies, Ann, surprised us at dinner with a PowerPoint presentation that satirized, in a very humorous way, my theme for the year, "Closing the gap between common sense and common practice." Important components of faculty "family" culture were highlighted in the presentation as a reminder to those who had been around for a while and as new insights to the almost half of the faculty who had been on board for five years or less. The presentation ended with everyone participating in a conga-line dance to Sister Sledge's hit song "We Are Family." These three "high priestesses," to use Terry Deal's term, did a lot to make Littleton High School a place where teachers wanted to be.

I cannot overstate the importance of humor in the workplace, and the principal helps set that tone by providing, or at least inviting, laughter. It is an important ingredient in making our high schools joyful and inviting places in which to work.

Vision and Direction

Surveys of teachers who leave a building, a district, or even the profession for reasons other than retirement reveal that a lack of clear expectations and feedback on performance regarding those expectations ranks high among the reasons for leaving. In an analysis of The National Association of Secondary School Principals' "breakthrough schools," high schools with at least 50 percent minority and free- and reduced-rate lunch populations and 90 percent graduation and college-acceptance rates, Howard Gradet (2006) made the following observation:

> Although there are a million reasons why some schools don't work, there's one thing that Breakthrough High Schools (BTHS) have in common: a principal who has a focused vision that is based on the need of his or her school and district and an ability to rally the troops and move the school away from the herd. (p. 16)

An ability to rally the troops around a needs-based vision is vital to the success of these schools. Vision and direction are critical to recruiting and retaining quality teachers.

The Direction 2000 years at Littleton High School were particularly powerful in this regard because the faculty had developed a common vision for the high school of the future, difficult as it was to implement. Teachers feel aimless and adrift in a school that lacks direction from leadership (teacher leaders and administrators) and has no unifying vision to tie the faculty, staff, students, and parent community together.

The issue of vision and direction is so important in leadership of high schools that an entire section is devoted to the topic later in this book.

Creating a Culture Open to Ideas

Early in my career as principal at Littleton High School, someone would ask from time to time, "Will there ever be a year around here when we don't have something new going on?" My answer was always a swift and unequivocal, "No, we are in the growth business, not the maintenance business."

I have had the opportunity to do consulting work in high schools around the country, and I can tell you that there are vast differences in school cultures on many fronts, but particularly with regard to openness to looking at and doing things differently. I recently presented a well-known and highly-regarded staff development program to the faculty of a medium-sized suburban high school who could not have been less interested in what I had to say. They were, for the most part, polite and courteous, but their body language communicated a loud and clear "we-don't-need-to-hear-any-of-this" message. Unfortunately, their student achievement data suggested otherwise. Or take the case of the school improvement teams from a rather large suburban district in California whose members were very open to new ideas and to change, but who were going back to school cultures that are so protective of the status quo and so hostile toward a genuine examination of school structures and practices that chances of successful implementation of the interventions I was presenting were next to none. In both of these cases, the culture of the school had to be worked on before school improvement initiatives would be able to take root. In both of these situations, and in others in which I have worked, I was glad that I was at Littleton High School.

What are the characteristics of a culture open to new ideas? What does such a culture look like in a comprehensive American high school? How does a school get there? What are the leadership possibilities here?

Learning Communities: A Culture Open to New Ideas

> "A high school will regard itself as a community in which members of the staff collaborate to develop and implement the school's learning goals."
>
> (*Breaking Ranks II*, 2004, p. 62)

Summarizing a definition put forth by T. MacNeil, Tu and Corry (2002), describe a learning community as "…a common place where people learn through group activity to define problems affecting them, to decide upon a solution, and to act to achieve the solution. As they progress, they gain new knowledge and skills" (p. 1). Peterson (2002), synthesizing the work of several writers and researchers, concludes that in schools with professional learning communities, the culture possesses the following values:

- ♦ "a widely shared sense of purpose and values;
- ♦ norms of continuous learning and improvement;

- a commitment to and sense of responsibility for the learning of all students;
- collaborative, collegial relationships; and
- opportunities for staff reflection, collective inquiry, and sharing personal practice." (p. 11)

Peterson defines school culture as "the set of norms, values and beliefs, rituals and ceremonies, symbols and stories that make up the 'persona' of the school" (p. 10). In Michael Fullan's words, "Reculturing is the name of the game" (2001, p. 34) for the kinds of schools I referenced earlier.

Several authors have defined and highlighted characteristics of school culture and its impact on student and adult learning. Peterson makes the following observations about the impact of positive and negative school culture:

- "When a school has a positive professional culture, one finds meaningful staff development, successful curricular reform, and the effective use of student performance data. In these cultures, staff and student learning thrive." (p. 10)
- "In contrast, a school with a negative or toxic culture that does not value professional learning, resists change, or devalues staff development hinders success. School culture will have either a positive or a detrimental impact on the quality and success of staff development." (p. 10)
- "Schools with toxic cultures lack a clear sense of purpose, have norms that reinforce inertia, blame students for lack of progress, discourage collaboration, and often have actively hostile relations among staff. These schools are not healthy for staff or students." (p. 11)
- "Being able to understand and shape the culture is key to a school's success in promoting staff and student learning." (p. 10)

In the ASCD publication, *Transforming Schools: Creating a Culture of Continuous Improvement*, Zmuda, Kuklis, and Kline (2004) speak similarly about important aspects of school culture in any educational reform effort:

- "context [that] not only matters, but forms the crucial backdrop for any serious enduring educational reform..." (p. vi)
- "the importance of changing minds, not just practices, through the messy processes of dialogue, debate, and reflection." (p. vi)
- "the need to reach a collective consensus on goals—internally embraced rather than externally imposed—combined with a shared ownership for results." (p. vi)
- "[the need] to structure the conversations and stimulate the reflections needed to unsettle the status quo and mobilize change." (p. vi)
- "shifts—from unconnected thinking to systems thinking, from an environment of isolation to one of collegiality, from perceived reality to

information-driven reality, and from individual autonomy to collective autonomy and collective accountability." (p. 1)

- ◆ "The school as a competent system [positive culture] has a shared vision that articulates a coherent picture of what the school will look like when its core beliefs are put into practice. It collects and synthesizes information on student achievement, identifies the gaps between current and desired performance, explores research and best practices to identify possible strategies or frameworks to enhance teacher practice, and then chooses an innovation or a bundled set of innovations to close the gap between where the school is and where it has to be to fulfill its vision. It has a staff development program and a related action plan that are necessary if the school is to achieve its shared vision. The program also must anticipate and take into account the predictable stages of teacher concerns about the complexities of moving from new learning to systemic consequences. In the process of building a competent system, the staff members emerge as a professional learning community, embracing collective accountability as the only way to achieve the shared vision for all students." (p. 1)
- ◆ "In a competent system, all staff members believe that what they have collectively agreed to do is challenging, possible, and worthy of the attempt." (p. 5)

Rick DuFour and Becky Burnette (2002) identify several steps that leaders can and must take in order to maintain a positive culture in a school. They suggest creating cognitive dissonance (tension or discomfort over the difference between what is and what ought to be), creating small victories to celebrate success along the way, cultivating effective teams focused on student achievement, providing time for collaboration, finding common ground to counter the tendency in high schools to protect turf, asking individuals and teams for commitment to whole-school reform, saying no to initiatives that spread the focus and work of school teams too thin, and developing targets and timelines to help school teams and the school as a whole maintain focus and direction (pp. 28–30).

Peterson (2002) also points out the importance of celebrating successes in staff meetings and ceremonies and recommends telling stories of accomplishments and collaboration whenever opportunities present themselves. In addition, he advocates using clear, shared language created during professional development to foster commitment to staff and student learning (p. 14).

The faculty at Littleton High School works hard every day to create a positive culture, a culture that exhibits the characteristics of a learning community, a culture open to ideas. The school's vision statement is used as a foundation for developing a sense of shared purpose. For example, a commitment to and sense of responsibility for the learning of all students is demonstrated, among other ways, by Littleton High School's development of both the International Baccalaureate program for highly-motivated students and the Freshman Academy for those at risk of failing. Dedication to building and maintaining collaborative, collegial relationships; to providing opportunities for staff reflection, collective inquiry, and sharing personal practice; and to nurturing norms of continuous learning and improvement is modeled by a staff development program that features departmental and interdepartmental collaborative critical reflection focused on student work.

The effort, planning, and vision that go into staff development work do a lot to build and maintain the kind of culture we need in our high schools. At Littleton High School, staff development time is never given over to teacher work time to catch up on grading or housekeeping chores. To do so would be to send the message that learning new skills and exploring ideas is not of high importance. The issues that a school leader talks about to individuals and to groups of teachers do a lot to build and maintain the kind of culture we need in our high schools. The extent to which a school leader is a reader, a thinker, and an explorer has a great deal of impact on the culture of the high school.

Few leadership functions are, in my opinion, more important than the responsibility for building and maintaining the kind of culture reflected in legitimate professional learning communities. Failure to attend to this matter limits growth for students, for teachers, and for the organization. Failure to do so makes high schools rather dull places in which to work.

Chapter 2

Creating a Vision That Teachers Want to Achieve

Creating a School Vision

I remember back in the mid 1980s when "creating a vision" was a relatively new thing, at least in education, and some veteran principals in our district and elsewhere were already growing weary of hearing about the "vision thing" all of the time. We were at a district meeting discussing contract benefits, including health benefits, for the next year when a veteran elementary principal said, "I don't know about this vision insurance. It hasn't protected us from one vision yet in this district."

Working with the school community, particularly with the school faculty, to create a vision for the school, a guiding statement that paints a picture of what it looks like when the school gets it right, is well accepted as an important high school leadership function, in spite of some humor to the contrary. It is an important component in the collaborative development of a professional learning community.

Struggling with the "Vision Thing" in Becoming a Learning Community

Howard Schultz, chairman and chief global strategist for Starbucks Coffee, understands the importance of vision: "Great companies are defined by their discipline and their understanding of who they are and who they are not...but also, great companies must have the courage to examine strategic opportunities that are transformational—as long as they are not inconsistent with the guiding principles and values of the core business"

(Overholt, 2004, p. 52). Schultz's statement on vision is a variation of Harvard Business School professor Theodore Levitt's question, "What business are you really in?" (p. 52). We would do well to apply the lessons from business to the operation of our schools. Schools, too, should consider these essential questions:

- What business are we in?
- What will schooling look like when we are truly accomplishing our mission?
- What is our vision for our school?

Coming up with a truly meaningful vision for a high school is very difficult because, among other things, of the pluralistic nature of most comprehensive high schools. High schools serve many interests, and it is not easy to get a school community to agree on the characteristics of effective schooling. Littleton High School has always had a vague institutional vision of a comprehensive high school where all students reach high academic standards and enjoy the high school "journey" along the way. But coming up with a unifying vision alluded the school community for many years.

Littleton High School's Vision Statement

Littleton High School's vision statement arose the natural way, coming out of our Direction 2000 school restructuring program in the late 1980s. Direction 2000 engaged the entire school community in rethinking the American high school, and that rethinking process forced us to deal with our overarching vision of a good education. Our vision statement was written by a group of teachers and has served to keep us grounded, particularly during difficult times. It has served the test of time by guiding us through numerous program changes. Direction 2000, the program which gave impetus to our vision statement, has evolved in many different ways, but the vision statement remains unchanged (Figure 2).

Opening ceremonies each year at Littleton High School include the reading of the Vision Statement to the faculty. Few things in the school's recent history, at least, have been as instrumental to building a culture of collaborative leadership, developing a sense of community, and creating a high school where teachers want to be than the development and regular renewal of a unique and compelling vision of learning.

Scenario Building

Vision statements alone are often not enough to provide the direction and sustained growth characteristic of healthy organizations. Members of

Figure 2

LITTLETON HIGH SCHOOL VISION STATEMENT

America needs young people who know how to learn, as well as how to read, write, speak, and compute. America needs young people with strong interpersonal skills, the ability to contribute to economic productivity and social progress and justice. America needs young people who can acquire, analyze, and apply information so as to think creatively and solve problems.

As workers, parents, citizens, and individuals, members of the next generation should know how to question, invent, anticipate, and dream.

We of the Littleton High School community should work every day to help young people do these things so that they can move, at last, beyond us, each prepared to make a living, make a life, and make a difference.

---

the school community, particularly teachers, need a common mental image of what the school, teaching, and learning will look like on a daily basis if the school's vision is actually realized. Alan Bersin, California Secretary of Education and former superintendent of the San Diego City Schools, put it this way: "People still don't give up what they know until you can project more clearly what it is you're going towards and what it is you want them to accomplish" (Collaborative Communications Group, Inc., 2006, p. 26).

There are many ways to lead a school community from a vision to a common mental image, but the one with which I have had the most success is scenario building. Littleton High School has gone through this exercise several different times and in several different ways over the past twenty years. During the Direction 2000 days, images of what an individualized, performance-based education would look like were written by faculty members and communicated to the school community through a project newsletter. Later, when the faculty was confused about the relationship among our building goals, staff development time was devoted to engaging interdisciplinary teams in constructing nonlinguistic representations of what it would look like if everything "fit together." The team presentations were clarifying, creative, and humorous.

In the fall of 2004, the faculty were again in need of a more concrete image of what an individualized, research-based, and project-focused education would look like on a day-in-and-day-out basis. This need arose, in part, from the fact that several new faculty members had been added in the last three years. At a two-day retreat in October (financed by private funds), the faculty members were handed a fictitious scenario about Littleton High School in the year 2010, similar to the one which follows (Figure 3).

Figure 3

SCENARIO FOR THE FUTURE
LITTLETON HIGH SCHOOL IN 2010

This scenario for the future is set against the background of homecoming week at Littleton High School in the year 2010. With the exception of the fact that today is droid dress-up day, all the other homecoming activities resemble those of ten years ago—athletic contests, the bonfire, the parade, the football game, etc. And like homecoming weeks of the past, the main topic of conversation among students this week is who is going with whom to Saturday night's dance.

But an examination of Littleton High School of 2010 reveals that many fundamental changes have occurred. For example, the school's focus, as played out in the daily activities of teachers and students, is not on dispensing information. Faculty and students believe that "facts themselves are no longer enough." Instead, education is research-based and product-focused. The traditional model of teaching has been turned on its head. No longer is it dominated by a one-size-fits-all, whole-group instruction mentality, with only occasional opportunities for students to engage in learning uniquely fitted to their particular interests, needs, and abilities. Now, students function as independent learners who come together on a regular basis to share, and often to debate, their learning. For students, education consists mostly of asking and answering questions. They are engaged in standards-based work that interests them.

Traditional whole-group instructional methods such as lectures and class discussion are still employed, of course. However, instead of dominating instruction as they used to, teachers utilize these techniques most often to introduce a new skill, concept, or unit of instruction, or to clarify common misunderstandings that emerge as students work. The expected ratio of individual and small-group work to whole-class instruction is roughly 2:1.

Student work reflects the faculty's efforts to integrate writing, information literacy, technology, and critical thinking into the curriculum. Written texts produced by students will quite likely include web logs, hypertexts, and entries into the students' electronic portfolios. Academic essays frequently include hyperlinks to connect readers to additional research, counter-arguments, or information that is relevant to the essay but not appropriate to include in the text itself. Research is used for more than just exploration. It is, in fact, the basis of learning for problem solving.

Littleton High School's Senior Year Plan partners teachers and students together to plan the second semester of each student's senior year. The goal of the program is to eliminate "senioritis" and instead to create a "launching pad" for seniors into college and/or a career.

Students and teachers begin to focus their thoughts on the upcoming student-parent-teacher conferences. Twice each year, students are required to present their

(cont'd.)

Figure 3 *(Continued)*

SCENARIO FOR THE FUTURE
LITTLETON HIGH SCHOOL IN 2010

---

portfolios to their parents with their teachers looking on. Each item in the electronic portfolio is referenced to a course, department, or academic standards or to a citizenship/work habit standard, so that parents and students can monitor progress toward mastery of a limited number of big ideas, course skills, and important habits of mind.

Faculty members recently convened for their monthly professional development planning meeting, which, like nearly all faculty conversations at Littleton High School, is about student work. These questions guide all of these discussions:

1. What do we want students to know?
2. How will we know if they are learning?
3. What are we going to do if they're not?

The Littleton High School faculty acknowledge that they still face a mountain of social, motivational, and academic challenges on a daily basis. Moving to a whole new level of performance will require more dramatic changes in purpose, structure, and practice than the Littleton community has thus far been willing to make. However, for 25 years, the vision at Littleton High School has been to prepare every student to make a living, make a life, and make a difference. With that as its continued goal, Littleton High School stands tall as a new American High School.

In interdisciplinary groups, the faculty was asked to respond to three questions:

♦ What about this scenario excites you in an I-wouldn't-want-to-miss-this kind of way?

♦ What would you add to or change about this scenario that would make it more compelling?

♦ Is this scenario, or the one you created, doable?

Department chairpersons and administrators discussed modifications to this scenario resulting from the retreat discussions at the following Curriculum Council meeting and decided to modify the scenario to include features such as a more flexible school day, the creation of student portfolios, and a community service graduation requirement.

That exercise really seemed to help move the faculty from a vision to a common mental image, an image which provided direction for our work and decision making. Figure 4, a policy for the use of technology at Littleton High

Figure 4

TECHNOLOGY AT LITTLETON HIGH SCHOOL

"Have a simple, clear purpose which gives rise to complex, intelligent behavior, rather than complex rules and regulations that give rise to simplistic thinking and stupid behavior." (Dee Hock, Founder, Visa)

Decisions about technology at Littleton High School (budget decisions, procurement decisions, distribution decisions, facilities decisions, staffing decisions, staff development decisions) should advance the following primary and secondary purposes of technology.

> **Primary Purpose:** To facilitate an individualized, research-based, and project-focused teaching and learning model.

> **Secondary Purpose:** To maximize the efficiency with which we do our work.

Other Values Affecting Technology Decision Making

1. **Equal Access:** Littleton High School has a socioeconomically diverse student population. A high value is placed on decisions that "level the playing field."

2. **Research Informed:** Whenever possible, technology decisions should be informed by what research and expert opinions tell us "works" vis-à-vis the aforementioned purposes of technology.

3. **Alignment with 4 Goals:** Technology decisions should further at least one of the four LHS goals.

4. **Effective Teaching:** When considering the purchase of new technology, we should base those decisions on what we know about best practice in the classroom.

School adopted by the Curriculum Council and the School Accountability Committee in 2005, is an example of this "direction."

Scenario building can unfold in various ways. Bob Barrows, former principal of Englewood High School in Englewood, Colorado, demonstrated excellent leadership and entrepreneurial skills by enlisting members of the Greater Denver arts community in producing a DVD that "painted a picture" of a proposed Englewood High School School of the Arts. The DVD and its accompanying brochure created a common mental image not only for potential funders, but also for members of the Englewood High School school community.

Part II

Leadership for Creating the High Schools of Our Choice

Chapter 3

What Teachers Must Do

"Leadership often involves challenging people to live up to their own words, to close the gap between their espoused values and their actual behavior" (Heifetz and Lensky, 2004, p. 33). With those words, Ronald Heifetz and Marty Lensky capture the essence of the leadership needed to create the high schools of our choice. So much of what high school principals and teacher-leaders do, or need to do, involves creating that cognitive dissonance, that creative dissatisfaction that moves people to confront the discrepancy between the kinds of schools we have and the kinds of schools our children deserve.

Closing the Gap

We hear a great deal these days about closing the gap—closing the achievement gap or closing the teaching gap, for example. That popular present-day call to action took on another meaning—a broader, more overarching meaning—for me in the summer of 2004 as I listened to Dr. Bertice Berry (2004) define the job of leadership in today's high schools in a keynote address as that of "closing the gap between common sense and common practice."

"Closing the gap between common sense and common practice..." I was struck that day by the simple elegance of that statement, elegance in the sense of a law of physics or proof in mathematics that explains so much of our world in so few words. For me, "closing the gap between common sense and common practice" has become the $E=MC^2$ of the high school principalship. Much of how we structure our schools and about how we conduct our day-to-day business runs counter to what we know "works" in schools and classrooms from the last thirty-five years of research in education and from our own common-sense experiences. In our more reflective moments, most of us acknowledge that some of the things we do in our schools do not make sense.

In my opening address to the faculty at the start of the 2004–05 school year, I identified eight of what I considered to be common sense "truths" facing the school at the time, along with the implications of those truths if we were to close the gap between common sense and common practice.

Common Sense...

♦ Students learn more when teachers and students are very clear about what the major outcomes of a lesson, a unit, and a course are and what "good work" looks like for each outcome.

♦ What a student can expect to learn and the "body of evidence" (student work) that will earn an A or a B in a course should not be determined by the teacher with whom the computer schedules that student.

Implications...

♦ We need to continue our work aimed at making sure our students know what good work looks like.

♦ We have more work to do before we will have "arrived" as a professional learning community, and we must do that work.

Common Sense...

♦ Students who leave high school unprepared to succeed in post-secondary education without remediation are at a disadvantage, probably for life.

Implication...

♦ We need to think of our mission as preparing all students for success (without remediation) in post-secondary education, not just getting into college.

Common Sense...

♦ Students who leave high school without strong reading, writing, math, and analytical thinking skills will not be successful in post-secondary education.

♦ Students will learn those skills best that are taught and applied multiple times by multiple teachers in multiple disciplines.

Implication...

♦ We must maintain focus on our power standards project as improving literacy advances our goals for student and teacher learning.

Common Sense...

♦ Students come to us with differences. If we expose them to the same "treatment," we will never close the achievement gap.

Implication...

♦ We must learn how to differentiate instruction in the high school setting.

Common Sense...

♦ If we see "dispensing information" as our only purpose, or even as our primary purpose, we will, and should, go out of business.

Implication...

♦ We need to talk more about a unifying purpose (mission) for our "comprehensive" school. We must walk with purpose.

Common Sense...

♦ Students are best served when teachers and administrators see their work as a personal calling, not just a job.

Implication...

♦ "My purpose is not my job; it's my calling." (Berry, 2004)

Later that same year (2004–05), I expanded the list for a keynote address on high school reform prepared for The Education Alliance at Brown University. Additional "common sense" practices to consider include the following:

♦ Curriculum anarchy is unfair to students. Thus, we need to identify a guaranteed and viable curriculum.

♦ Too many standards spoil the schools. Thus, we need to identify essential learning.

♦ Remedial classes increase the achievement gap. We must work to devise better ways to help those who have been left behind to catch up with their peers.

♦ If literacy is the responsibility of the language arts department only, the students will never learn to read the handwriting on the wall. Thus, we need a broad literacy goal extending across all disciplines.

♦ If the only arrow in your dealing-with-at-risk-students quiver is to change the kids rather than to change the system, you will end up shooting yourself in the foot. Our Freshman Academy is designed to instigate change in the system.

♦ Education without personal meaning results in little more than end-of-the-unit data dumps. This is the basis of our argument for a constructivist learning theory.

♦ You cannot teach big ideas in little snippets of time. Block scheduling gives us the time we need to teach important concepts and big ideas.

♦ High school is neither the beginning nor the end of life. The high schools of our choice will feature effective ninth and twelfth grade transitions programs.

- "Senioritis" is not going to go away as long as the eighth semester of high school continues to look just like the other seven. We must develop programs and options that make the senior year a transition to life after high school.
- The current "Prego approach" to grading renders grades meaningless. We must move to standards-based grading.
- We cannot afford to lose 50 percent of new teachers in the first five years of teaching. We should establish mentoring, coaching, and induction programs.
- "Inbreeding does not give birth to genius." We must broaden our professional learning communities.
- "Drive-by" staff development never has and never will work. We must insist upon a goals-driven, ongoing system of professional development.
- Data-driven (as opposed to data-informed and values-driven) decision making lacks soul. We must keep our priorities clearly grounded.
- We will never be as good as we can be, or as good as we need to be, as long as the ruling metaphor for the American high school is "a collection of educational entrepreneurs held together by a common parking lot." We must collaborate more effectively.
- Real change takes time. We must keep that in mind instead of seeking quick fixes for our problems.

How does my list compare with the list for the school with which you are most familiar?

Teacher Leadership and School Improvement: Closing the Gap between Common Sense and Common Practice

"Teachers will provide the leadership essential to the success of reform, collaborating with others in the education community to redefine the role of the teacher and to identify sources of support for that redefined role."
(*Breaking Ranks II*, 2004, p. 63)

Much of this section of the book on leadership deals with leadership by the school principal. However, before going there, we must recognize and explore the notion of distributed leadership. There is near universal agreement among both researchers and practitioners that the high school principal can not do it alone. There is also widespread agreement that teacher leadership is critical to substantive school improvement.

Bertice Berry's suggestion that the challenge of school leadership is one of closing the gap between common sense and common practice can be used as a framework to explore the importance of teacher leadership and the connection between teacher leadership and school improvement.

Common sense and research tell us that human beings—not programs, initiatives, systems, movements, or devices—guarantee progress and that student learning depends first, last, and always on the quality of the teachers in our schools (Ferguson, 1991; Sanders and Rivers, 1996; Marzano, 2003, p. 74). Former San Diego superintendent Alan Bersin describes the theory of action that he and colleague Tony Alvarado held regarding improving high schools:

> The critical path for improving student achievement, especially for poor kids, is to improve the quality of teaching. Other people will talk about other elements of the San Diego reform, but our central focus was how to improve teaching at scale.... The most sure-fire way to improve KT–12—including the high school—would be by improving the quality of teaching across the board.... It's not about structure: It's about instruction." (Collaborative Communications Group, Inc., 2006, pp. 1–2)

Yet common practice is that much of what goes on in the name of "school reform" does not put teaching and learning at the center of the initiative. Such initiatives are destined to fail. Richard Elmore (2003) from Harvard describes the qualities essential to the success of reform initiatives:

> Successful leaders...understand that improving school performance requires transforming a fundamentally weak instructional core, and the culture that surrounds it, into a strong, explicit body of knowledge about powerful teaching and learning that is accessible to those who are willing to learn it." (p. 9)

Bersin observes that the fact that the Carnegie Corporation and the Gates Foundation see themselves as catalysts of high school reform "is a remarkable reflection of the weak knowledge base in our [the education] sector" (Collaborative Communications Group, Inc., 2006, p. 21). The first question, then, that instructional leaders must ask themselves centers on the focus of school reform: "Is improving teaching and learning the focus of the school improvement initiatives underway at our school?"

Research and common sense also describe for us the kind of culture needed in schools for sustainable school improvement. It is a culture that can only be created with significant teacher leadership. Recall the earlier reference (repeated here in abbreviated form) to the characteristics that Zmuda, Kuklus, and Kline (2004) identify as important to a culture that nurtures growth:

♦ "the need to reach a collective consensus on goals—internally embraced rather than externally imposed—combined with a shared ownership of results." (p. vi)

♦ "the importance of changing minds, not just practices, through the messy processes of dialog, debate, and reflection." (p. vi)

- "[the need] to structure the conversations and stimulate the reflections needed to unsettle the status quo and mobilize change." (p. vi)
- "shifts—from unconnected thinking to systems thinking, from an environment of isolation to one of collegiality, from perceived reality to information-driven reality, and from individual autonomy to collective autonomy and collective accountability." (p. 1)

Who or what can make that happen? Administrators and school board members, structures, time, and resources are all important to the "re-culturing" of the school. But only teachers can make it happen.

Common practice, on the other hand, is that teacher leadership is often confined to activities—department chairperson, union representative, committee member—tangential to the core of the profession. Defining what good teaching is and exerting control over the quality of teaching and learning are tasks most often left to administrators and politicians. For example, instructional walkthroughs, a strategy used increasingly to identify and reflect upon good teaching practice, is seldom done by teachers. In a national survey conducted by Beldon, Russonello, and Stewart for *Education Week* (2005), 96 percent of superintendents said principals did the walkthroughs, 46 percent said they were done by central office staff, and only 20 percent said teachers participated in instructional walkthroughs. (*From the Top*, p. 37). Therefore, a second question for instructional leaders centers on the scope of teacher leadership: "What does teacher leadership look like in our school?"

Common sense tells us that we need a new kind of teacher leadership in our high schools if we expect to improve significantly student performance in all student groups. That means that teaching must become a genuine profession rather than one still seeking public legitimacy. In a profession, leadership and quality control come from within.

I am not suggesting that teachers, as individuals, do not act "professionally." The vast majority of teachers with whom I have worked over the years conduct themselves with students and with parents, and attend to their individual professional growth, in a manner that we generally associate with the professions. But the concept of individual teachers acting "professionally" is not the same as teaching as a profession. And all we have to do is reflect for just a second on, let's say, "professional wrestling" to know that simply calling one's work a profession does not make it so. Professions exhibit certain characteristics that distinguish them from other worthwhile vocational pursuits.

In a study for the Aspen Institute, Judy Wurtzel (2006) identifies seven elements of professionalism that are common across all sectors:

- "A professional owes her *primary duty to her clients.*
- Professionals are *accountable to the profession for results.* . . . Each profession has a definition of malpractice and the profession itself has

standards and procedures for sanctioning and ultimately ejecting from the profession those who commit malpractice.

♦ In each profession there exists a *body of specialized knowledge and agreed upon standards of practice and specific protocols for performance. . . .* These norms and protocols are based on either evidence of effectiveness in improving results for clients or...codified agreement by the profession about practices and protocols most likely to benefit clients.

♦ A professional has a *duty to improve her own practice.*

♦ A professional has a *duty to improve common or collective practice* in the profession.

♦ Professionals are expected to *exercise professional judgment* . . . [and] to consider the specific characteristics and needs of their clients [when applying the standards and protocols of the profession].

♦ Professionals . . . *must seek to foster productive client behaviors that lead to successful outcomes.* They cannot mandate compliance . . ." (pp. 7–8)

Wiggins and McTighe (2006) provide us with a somewhat shorter but nonetheless complementary list of characteristics of professionals that can also be used to evaluate the extent to which teaching is a profession. According to these authors, professionals do the following:

♦ "act on the most current knowledge that defines their field,

♦ are client-centered and adapt to meet the needs of the individuals whom they serve,

♦ are results-oriented, and

♦ uphold the standards of the profession in their own practice and through peer review." (p. 28)

How does the field of teaching stack up? Do high school teachers act on current knowledge, or are teaching strategies employed because they are familiar regardless of what research says about their effectiveness? Is a duty to improve the collective practice of other teachers in the profession and in the district and school in which one works a widely held cultural norm? Do the norms of the field dictate that decisions—about master schedules, teaching assignments, course offerings, and instructional outcomes, for example—be made based on what is best for kids rather than on what makes teachers feel most comfortable? Are high school teachers typically quick to differentiate instruction to meet the needs of individual students? Historically, has good teaching been defined by inputs or results; by what has been taught or by what has been learned? Is peer review the primary method by which the standards of good teaching are upheld, and are teachers ejected from the profession by teachers if they commit malpractice?

Richard Elmore (2003) answers those questions in his own way:

> Educators are subject to draconian and dysfunctional external accountability policies largely because they have failed to develop strong and binding professional norms about what constitutes high-quality teaching practice and a supportive educational environment. . . . Internal coherence around instructional practice is a prerequisite for strong performance. (p. 8)

In speaking of "draconian and dysfunctional external accountability policies" could Elmore be talking about NCLB legislation and similar state accountability policies, and is he suggesting that we did it to ourselves?

In a report for the Aspen Institute advocating for the "professionalization" of teaching, Judy Wurtzel (2006) asserts that "Today, educators often define professionalism as freedom to make their own decisions about what, how, and sometimes even whom to teach" (p. 7). Bess Keller, in an article for *Education Week,* reports the dissatisfaction of many educators who attended the inaugural meeting of the recently formed TeacherSolutions project, an effort by the Center for Teacher Quality in Chapel Hill, N.C., to bring teachers' voices to the education-policy debate. One speaker, Jennifer Morrison, an award-winning teacher from North Carolina, said, "Teachers aren't expected to think beyond their own students or buildings—in fact, leading or contributing to the profession as a whole is discouraged because it takes teachers out of the classroom." At that same event, a teacher from Florida confessed that "all teachers are not doing the same job, [but] I can't say that at a faculty meeting." Ford Morishita, a biology teacher from Oregon and another TeacherSolutions participant reminded colleagues that school change agents would be "fighting 'a culture and a mindset' that mistrusts any behavior that distinguishes one teacher from another." (Keller, 2006, p. 7). Alan Bersin, speaking of his experiences as superintendent in San Diego, describes the system more harshly: "I have never seen a service sector. . . that combines fiscal allocations, political accommodations and cultural views in such a manner as to produce results that are so oriented toward the provider's interests rather than the needs and desires of our customers—our students and their parents" (Collaborative Communications Group, Inc., 2006, p. 24).

The formation of The National Board of Professional Teaching Standards was one response to the need to professionalize teaching. Bess Keller (2006) recently reported the words of James B. Hunt, former North Carolina governor and chair of the board for its first decade: "The [NBPTS] was originally set up to try to help create a true profession of teaching because we didn't agree on standards, and we didn't assess teachers rigorously, and we didn't have ways to move them along in the profession" (p. 14). And James A. Kelly, president of the NBPTS during its first 12 years, supported Hunt's analysis by saying, "[The organization's board] was the broadest group ever brought together in the history of [American] education. [The standards it approved amounted to] a historic statement for what good teaching should be and represented a remarkable consensus" (p. 14).

Board-certified teachers in Miami gave us some idea of what teaching as a profession might look like when they announced their intention to be at the fore of the school improvement agenda in that district: "We're going to take an active and assertive role in doing what should be done for all the children in the district.... changing the dynamics of the discussion by being the ones to champion teacher quality" (Keller, 2005, p. 19). "Teachers as champions of teacher quality"— now that's starting to sound like a profession. The Teacher Leader Network, another project of the Center for Teaching Quality that electronically connects 300 teachers to help them advocate for effective teaching practices, is another budding attempt to "professionalize" the field. But these forays into professionalism are few and far between.

The Institute for Educational Leadership in Washington, D.C. (http://www.iel.org/) has offered five different definitions of teacher leadership in a recent roundtable discussion among education policy analysts (see Figure 5). These definitions provide a good starting point for a school-based discussion of teacher leadership.

So the next two questions instructional leaders can ask about teacher leadership are (1) "Is teaching a profession at our school?" and (2) "Does a collaboratively-developed definition or vision of teacher leadership exist at our school?"

In *The World is Flat*, Thomas Freidman (2005) pulls together data from both the public and the private sectors worldwide to support the conclusion that vertical hierarchies in organizations are giving way to horizontal information-sharing networks and collective decision making (pp. 175–181). Such a shift would also benefit our schools: horizontal hierarchies, teachers working with teachers sharing state-of-the-art information and making decisions collectively guided by agreed-upon standards and protocols, not vertical hierarchies with bureaucrats telling teachers what's good practice and what isn't. Doug Reeves (2006) makes the point that the process of change in schools is dominated by a belief in rational thinking, a belief that rational argument changes teacher behavior (p. 33). In other words, all I have to do as principal is cover the faculty with statistics about the superiority of a particular teaching practice or program, and, having seen the light, teachers will make the desired adjustments in their classrooms. Instead, Reeves argues that teachers are influenced to change what they do by the words and actions of trusted colleagues. In other words, teachers learn from other teachers, not from administrators sharing what they heard at a recent conference. Reeves labels these influential colleagues "hubs" and "superhubs"—people at the points of connectivity in schools (p. 34). As high school principals and their leadership teams think about teacher leadership in the pursuit of school improvement, they should be asking these

Figure 5

DEFINITIONS OF TEACHER LEADERSHIP

Definition 1

"A teacher leader is like Galileo: a maverick who learns as much as he can about his field, envisions what others can not see, questions provincial wisdom, and holds up against a system that rewards mediocrity and resists change. He remains committed to what he believes is right, works for the good of his students, and endeavors to influence those on the district, state, and national levels."

Definition 2

"A teacher leader is a proficient handler of curriculum matters in the classroom. From the classroom she emerges to share ideas, collaborate with others, and influence issues that affect students, teachers, and schools. The teacher leader sees the classroom as the best starting point to institute change."

Definition 3

"A teacher leader has credibility, starting with a solid background in his subject and how to teach it, as well as the inclination and structures to learn more. He is flexible with his thinking, well read, freely exchanges ideas and critiques with others, and he discussed education issues knowledgeably. He fights complacency in both his classroom and his community, and he is willing to express his opinion in a manner in which it is heard by others. He is willing to take risks to reach his and his institution's goals. He is reflective and able to see the 'big picture.'"

Definition 4

"Teacher leaders make their teaching and learning public through their collaborative and reflective practice. Teacher leaders document their thinking and practice in order to deepen their learning and hold themselves accountable. Teacher leaders consistently push the hard questions of equity and achievement and keep all students at the center of their decision making."

Definition 5

"The actions of the teacher leader are always driven by the desire to advocate for children. Teacher leaders are proactive and seek opportunities to improve public education at the school, district, state, and national levels. Teacher leaders are effective communicators and collaborators. Teacher leaders find innovative means to stay informed about issues in education and seek to understand those issues from their own context and extend that understanding to the broader educational context to influence policy."

From Norton, John. "Our First Conversation: What Does It Mean to Be a Teacher Leader?" *Teacher Leaders Network* (March 24–26, 2003); with permission. Available at: http://www.teacherleaders.org/images/chat1excpt.pdf

essential questions: (1) "Who are the hubs and superhubs in our building?" and (2) "Are they at the center of the change process?"

Professional learning communities, properly designed and supported, embody this notion of horizontal information-sharing networks, of teachers learning from other teachers, and of teaching as a profession. Professional learning communities increase social capital. As Harvard professor and author of *Bowling Along*, Robert Putnam (2000), stated at an economic summit, "The basic idea of social capital is that networks have value...for transmitting information...for undergirding cooperation and reciprocity." It is little wonder that Rick and Becky Dufour (2004) identify building the capacity of school personnel to function as professional learning communities as the most promising strategy for sustained, substantial school improvement (2004 Denver workshop). It's common sense. But common practice is that professional learning communities in too many schools exist in name only because of a lack of teacher ownership and leadership. To what extent are professional learning communities in your school "professional?"

A final question to consider when seeking to develop and nurture teacher leadership and channeling that leadership toward sustained, substantive school improvement is, "Are our teacher leaders working on the right stuff?" In *The Seven Habits of Highly Effective People*, Stephen Covey (1989) writes, "If the ladder is not leaning against the right wall, every step we take just gets us to the wrong place faster" (p. 98). In a similar vein, in *School Leadership That Works*, Marzano, Waters, and McNulty (2005) argue that the problem with low-performing schools often is not that they are not working hard, but rather that they are working on the wrong stuff. (Marzano, Waters, and McNulty, p. 76) In my experience, there are only two ways to get better results: redesign your school based on best practices or get different kids. If you have the option of getting better kids (perhaps parents are hiding the good ones from you), read no further. If not, however, then research-based best practices are what teacher leaders should be working on.

Bob Marzano (2003) provides one such reference point in *What Works in Schools: Translating Research into Theory*. In that book, Marzano identifies eleven research-based factors that influence student academic achievement (Figure 6). That would be an excellent place for a team of teacher leaders to begin. For example, working in subject matter, course, or grade-level teams, teachers could identify a district's or a school's "guaranteed and viable curriculum" and "challenging goals and effective feedback strategies" (Factors 1 & 2). Factor 5, "Collegiality and Professionalism," obviously calls for teacher leadership. "Instructional Strategies," Factor 6, gets at the core of school improvement and capitalizes on Reeves' observation that teachers learn new behaviors from other teachers. Teacher leadership is needed in identifying the academic vocabulary that students need to master by subject and by grade level in order to be successful in school (Factor 10, "Learned Intelligence and

Figure 6

FACTORS INFLUENCING ACHIEVEMENT	
School	1. A guaranteed and viable curriculum
	2. Challenging goals and effective feedback
	3. Parent and community involvement
	4. Safe and orderly environment
	5. Collegiality and professionalism
Teacher	6. Instructional strategies
	7. Classroom management
	8. Classroom curriculum design
Student	9. Home environment
	10. Learned intelligence/background knowledge
	11. Student motivation

From Marzano, Robert J. *What Works in Schools: Translating Research into Action.* Alexandria, VA: ASCD, 2003, p. 10. Reprinted by Permission. The Association for Supervision and Curriculum Development is a worldwide community of educators advocating sound policies and sharing best practices to achieve the success of each learner. To learn more, visit ASCD at www.ascd.org.

Background Knowledge"). In fact, it is easy to argue that each of Marzano's eleven factors require teacher leadership to maximize results. The point is that by working on one or more of these factors, a school improvement team would know that its ladder is leaning against the right, or at least a right, wall. That's common sense. Common practice is that too many teachers are busy working on the wrong things.

What would teacher leadership look like if teaching became a profession? At least two organizations have painted rather clear pictures of the kinds of questions teachers would be asking and the kinds of things teacher would be doing if teacher leadership was defined as it has been described here. The following questions for teacher leaders are presented in materials from the Institute for Educational Leadership (2001) in Washington D.C.:

♦ "How can we create the 'professional community' that research shows is essential to peak school and student performance?

♦ How can we create a school environment where each student is known and treated as an individual?

♦ What can be done to increase the quality of teachers and enhance the professionalism of teaching and teachers?

♦ How can the necessary bridge be made between challenging academic standards and accountability and what goes on in the classroom?

- What can be done to ensure that state and national policies to reform education are informed by the realities of the school and the classroom...?" (p. 4)

Teacher leaders should also consider what teachers can do to create curriculum and instruction that pushes all students to high levels of proficiency and how they can demonstrate the belief that all students can learn.

The Aspen Institute's publication *Transforming High School Teaching and Learning* is also an excellent source of rich descriptions of what teacher leadership in teaching as a profession might look like. For example, teachers would be "engaged in planned inquiry, research and evaluation to continually improve their own and the profession's knowledge and use of effective practices." And "...participation in professional development, coaching, classroom observation and continued learning is an essential part of the teaching job, not an optional activity. 'Going public' with student learning data and classroom practice is a core value that teachers share and incorporate into their own practice and their work with other teachers" (Wurtzel, 2006, pp. 9–10). The argument for teacher leadership as a necessary component of school reform is summed up in the following Aspen Institute vision of teacher leadership:

> In this vision, teachers' commitment to improving student outcomes and their individual and collective practice positions them as central actors in developing the school and district-wide infrastructure for instructional improvement. Teachers serve as developers and evaluators of their tools of practice—curriculum, assessment, lesson plans, professional development—and feed a school-wide, district-wide and profession-wide effort to increase knowledge and improve practice. Teacher autonomy is not a value or goal in itself. Instead, it is a resource for improvement. (p. 10)

To be fair, teachers haven't gotten the support from administrators, policy makers, and unions they need to become professionals. An article in *Education Week* reports on speculation that a number of union leaders who have recently been voted out of office by their memberships have lost their jobs, in part, because they worked too collaboratively with district leaders in promoting school reform (Honawar, 2006). That itself may be a reflection on how far teaching has to come in becoming a profession.

Administrators and policy makers have a roll to play in moving teaching to a professional status as well. They must insure that

- Teaching and learning are the focus of school improvement efforts,
- Teacher leadership is redefined, moving away from a primarily managerial/administrative mentality,
- Networks, hubs and superhubs are recognized, identified and placed at the center of the school improvement process,

- Teachers act as professionals and that administrators and policy makers provide the training and the support necessary for them to do so,
- A vision of teacher leadership is collaboratively developed at each district and school,
- Professional Learning Communities advance the cause of professionalism in our schools, and
- Our professionals are working on the right stuff.

Teacher leadership for school improvement is common sense, but not yet common practice.

Personal Learning Plans

> "Every school will be a learning community for the entire community. As such, the school will promote the use of Personal Learning Plans for each educator and provide the resources to ensure that the principal, teachers, and other staff members can address their own learning and professional development needs as they relate to improved student learning."
> (*Breaking Ranks II*, 2004, p. 63)

In schools and districts where teaching is a profession, teachers take ownership in their own professional growth and in the growth of their colleagues. The traditional model of supervision, evaluation, and goal setting-a model which I perpetuated for more than a decade at Littleton High School-is based on the hierarchical model which puts the administrator in charge and places the teacher in a passive, even subservient, role. Members of my administrative team and I would observe classes and essentially tell teachers what was good practice and what wasn't. Near the end of the supervision/evaluation process, teachers were engaged in a discussion of potential professional growth goals for the next evaluation cycle, but the administrator still held the trump card because the professional growth goals were expected to flow from the summative evaluation. Under this model, the administrator "owned" the process and its products and did most of the work. This process has some validity and meaning for new teachers and for veteran teachers who are on improvement plans. Veteran teachers in good standing, on the other hand, need only comply with the requirements of the growth plan without having to make any substantial changes in teaching behaviors. The most obvious indicator to me of the superficiality of this process occurred during annual reviews of professional growth goals because teachers often struggled to remember what they had turned in the previous spring. Nervous laughter was all most of them could come up with.

Appendix 6 in *Breaking Ranks II* outlines in some detail the professional growth planning model that Littleton High School developed and began implementing in the late 1990s. The three-year Professional Learning Plan is an option available only to teacher-status employees (nonprobationary teachers). During year one teachers reflect on their philosophy of teaching and, in consultation with their supervisor and a colleague of their choosing, identify their professional growth goal or goals and expected outcomes for the cycle. During year two of the three-year cycle, teachers actually carry out the growth activities outlined during the planning phase the previous year. The range of possible activities in which teachers can be involved is wide open and includes action research, peer coaching, cognitive coaching, data collection and analysis, and the design of quality work for students. Teachers are expected to document progress toward the previously-agreed-upon growth goal or goals. Year three is the period for reflection. Teachers construct a narrative of how what they learned will be incorporated into their teaching. An outline of the activities for each year is shown in Figure 7).

With this model, the teacher plays the lead role and does most of the work. The evaluator does approve the plan and sign off on its completion and conduct one classroom observation and follow-up conference. There is

Figure 7

TIMELINE		
Date	**Activity**	**Submitted to**
October 6, 2004	Inform evaluator about your decision.	Designated Evaluator
December 13, 2004	Complete: Philosophy of Effective Teaching and Learning	Designated Evaluator
April 15, 2005	Complete: Collaborative Professional Worksheet and The Learning Plan	Designated Evaluator
April 18–29	Meet with your evaluator to refine the plan.	NA
May 6, 2005	Submit The Learning Plan. Both parties sign The Learning Plan Report.	Designated Evaluator
August, 2005– May, 2006	Execute the growth opportunities outlined in The Learning Plan.	NA
January 30, 2007	Complete: My Final Thoughts	Designated Evaluator

no summative evaluation report. In addition to *Breaking Ranks II*, an excellent resource for designing and implementing personal learning plans, entitled *Personal Learning Plans for Educators*, is available from the National Association of Secondary School Principals (Webb and Berkbuegler, 1998).

Not every teacher chooses this option, although most do. A few teachers prefer to play a passive role and let the administrator do all the work. Most, however, prefer to be treated as professionals. If we want teaching to be a profession, common sense tells us that putting teachers in charge of their professional growth must become common practice.

Chapter 4

What Principals and Central Office Administrators Must Do

The Role of the Principal

"The principal will provide leadership in the school community by building and maintaining a vision, focus, and direction for student learning."

(*Breaking Ranks II*, 2004, p. 61)

The common sense notion that leadership matters is well supported by research (Leithwood and Riehl, 2003, p. 4; Marzano, Waters, and McNulty, 2005, p. 10). In fact, leadership is second only to quality teaching among school-related factors in its impact on student learning. The principal who, with his or her leadership team, has successfully led his or her school community in closing the gap between common sense for that community and common practice in that community can feel good about having provided the leadership needed to create the high schools of our choice.

What are the attitudes, characteristics, habits of mind, and skills needed to lead in today's high schools? Reflecting on my experiences, I believe there are certain principal behaviors that distinguish the leader from the manager.

Scholarship

If we expect teachers to exhibit the characteristics of a profession, and if we accept the notion that professionals keep abreast of new developments in their field, then principals must model that behavior. Leaders in today's high schools needs to be well educated, well read, and well informed. In short, high school principals need to be scholars.

What does scholarship look like for a high school principal? For one thing, it means that the principal is perhaps the best-read professional in the building on a wide variety of topics related to high school education. That reading should include, at the very least, a variety of education periodicals, journals, and books, but ideally would also include reading from outside the field of education. *Effective Literacy Instruction: Building Successful Reading and Writing Programs*, by Judith A. Langer (2002), was on my reading list in 2004 in support of our building literacy goal. Topics from the business world—for example, change theory, organizational development, leadership, culture building, and trend analysis—not only build leadership skills but also help the principal lead the school community in creating a school vision that is future oriented. And it is not enough that the leader be well read. He or she must also share what is learned from that reading with members of the education community, particularly with the school's faculty, in ways that meet the needs of each separate audience.

Scholarship for a high school principal also means learning with others by attending conferences, workshops, training sessions, and professional development meetings wherein, once again, issues related to where our world is headed and where our high schools should be headed are analyzed and discussed. Collaborative critical reflection is important for leaders too.

Research is also part of scholarship for today's educational leader; therefore, educational leaders in today's high schools must be comfortable using technology to access and evaluate the wealth of research and professional literature available to inform decision making. A person who is technophobic will not be viewed as the school's leading scholar by today's students, teachers, and parents.

The excuse is often made that the busy high school principal does not have time for professional reading and for the other acts of scholarship recommended in these pages. I disagree. Indeed, high school principals are busy people. Seventy-hour work weeks are not unusual. But no matter how busy we are, we must find time for those activities of highest priority. Scholarship needs to be on that list. We are, after all, in charge of a school, an educational institution, an organization devoted to learning. Lack of scholarship on the part of a high school principal, in my opinion, leaves too large a gap between our words and our behaviors.

My preferred avenues for learning and scholarship are professional reading and attendance at conferences and workshops. My regular reading list includes *Education Week*, *Educational Leadership* (ASCD), *Principal Leadership* (NASSP), and the *Kappan*. I also try to work in at least a couple of books during the summer, usually on topics of leadership and/or organizational development. I have found workshops and conferences by NASSP and ASCD, as well as those by our own state organization, the Colorado Association of School Executives (CASE), to be generally well run and worthwhile. I also conduct workshops for both NASSP and ASCD.

There are few shortcuts to scholarship. It takes time, and that time must find its way onto the priority list for the busy high school principal.

A Focus on Teaching and Learning

Managers focus on office paperwork and on keeping the building running. Leaders, of course, must perform some management functions, but they focus the majority of their time on issues and work related directly to teaching and learning.

As a high school principal, I worked hard at establishing structures—mechanisms, routines, habits, and expectations—that would assist me in devoting the majority of my time on the job to building and maintaining culture and monitoring and improving instruction. When I was away from the building, I carried no cell phone or pager. I did not call the school to find out what was going on. There were several reasons for this approach on my part, not the least of which was that I had very competent assistants who were perfectly capable of dealing with anything that might come up on a day-to-day basis. But the "bottom line" reason for my relative freedom was that I did not do anything that had to do with the day-to-day running of the building. In fact, when the time came to explain administrative functions to our new recruits during new teacher orientation each year, we often joked about the paucity of duties (none, actually) listed under my name.

My focus was on what was going on in the classrooms and in the halls. I spent my time visiting classrooms, two to three hours at a time, on at least three days each week. I spent my time talking with individuals and small groups of teachers about matters of teaching and learning. I tried to stay out of the office as I learned early on in my career that people with problems tend to show up there. If I wasn't available, either someone else would help them, or, if the issue was really important, they would come back later, allowing time for the emotions of the moment to subside a bit. Much of my time was spent with small teams—committees, planning teams, the administrative team—working on various aspects of organizational development. Long-term professional development planning is an example of the latter. Some of my time was devoted to external relations, particularly with our parent groups. During the second semester of each school year, I spent a great deal of time interviewing perspective teachers and conducting reference checks on those candidates to ensure that the professionals in our school were among the best in the nation and that they were a good "match" for Littleton High School.

Of course, I did occasionally have to meet with the unhappy parent or get involved in a sensitive expulsion case. And if I saw things related to our facility or grounds that did not meet my standards, I saw to it that someone took care of those things. But the time I spent with unhappy parents, discipline cases, facility matters, and the like occupied less than ten percent of my time.

I recognize that each situation is unique and that not every high school principal has the resources and support I had at Littleton High School. For example, assistant principals may not be as available as were mine, or even exist. And in these post-Columbine days superintendents often insist that principals carry pagers or cell phones. Still, with local considerations and expectations taken into account, the bottom line remains the same. The leaders of the kinds of high schools we want must demonstrate a commitment to focusing on teaching and learning, and that commitment must be reflected in the way they spend their time.

Delegation

One of the reasons I was able to spend my time focusing on teaching and learning is that I am a master delegator. I have already mentioned that in assigning duties to members of the administrative team, I did not assign myself anything that had to do with the management or day-to-day operation of the school. My assistant principals, my athletic director, and my secretary took care of all of that. When I delegate responsibility, I delegate the authority that goes with it. Staff members cannot be expected to show initiative and to own decisions if the principal is constantly looking over their shoulders and second-guessing their decisions. I did not overturn decisions made by assistants, even when I disagreed with them. To do so would have seriously undermined their credibility with the faculty and staff. Instead, we talked privately about how a similar matter might be handled differently the next time around.

I also encouraged assistants to take ownership for their decisions. Every time one of them said to a faculty or staff member, "I don't know, you had better ask Tim," it sent the message to that faculty or staff member that the assistant wasn't empowered to do much of anything, but rather acted only as a puppet to the principal. A better strategy is that the assistant make the decision, or. at the very least, say something like, "I need to think about that and get back to you," gaining the assistant time to confer in private with the principal. Delegation will not work if those to whom duties are delegated are not seen as empowered decision makers. And a focus on teaching and learning on the part of the principal will not happen without delegation.

The Importance of Longevity

One of the biggest obstacles to long-term school improvement is the all too common two- or three-year in and out rotation of principals in our high schools. Change takes time and requires continuity in leadership. Speaking at The Association for Supervision and Curriculum Development's 2006 Annual Conference, Andy Hargreaves, Thomas More Brennan Chair in the Lynch School of Education at Boston College, told principals that to make an impact, they have to stay in a position for at least five years (Scherer, 2006, p. 7). Mel Riddle, principal of J. E. B. Stuart High School in Fairfax County, Virginia, and 2005 NASSP/Met Life Principal of the Year, is aware of the important role time plays in significant school improvement: "It takes three, five, six, eight years [for change to occur]" (Gradet, 2006, pp. 19–20). In his response to a question about why it was important that he stay in San Diego for seven years, Alan Bersin estimated an even longer time frame to establish the consistent leadership necessary to institute change: "Continuity of vision and effort. Nobody is indispensable. Nonetheless, maintenance, development of capacity and expectations and providing people with room and time to grow into change requires continuity.... If you think you can smash that process of change into a two-year period, you're wrong.... We have completed the first phase of the reform in San Diego and it took every bit of seven years. I believe it is a 20-year process that proceeds in stages" (Collaborative Communications Group, Inc., 2006, p. 23).

I will not go so far as to say that a leader cannot make any difference at all in a year or two. I have seen examples of high school principals who have significantly improved the climate of the school in less than three years. But any kind of long-term school improvement, the kind that might last when the principal moves on, is going to take at least three to five years. In fact, many of the initiatives described at Littleton High School have been underway in a formal manner for a decade or more, with the roots of some programs going back as far as twenty years. Developing a broad leadership base in a high school is important; the principal cannot and should not do it alone. But teachers cannot be expected to invest in a significant school improvement effort if the history of the school suggests that principals—and therefore support for initiatives—come and go every couple of years.

Of course, situations sometimes necessitate a shorter tenure than the principal had anticipated when first taking a job. Some superintendents and school boards turn out to be not worth working for. And sometimes professional opportunities come at unexpected times. In my own case, my first principalship lasted only two years because an opportunity for me to return to school full time to complete my doctorate presented itself earlier than I had expected. But generally, a person should not take a principalship with the intent of serving for only a couple of years before moving on to something "bigger and better." Successful careers are usually not marked with a long list of positions where many initiatives were begun but few were finished. Instead, successful careers belong to those leaders who found someplace where they could make a difference and stuck with it.

Compensation packages and contracts should be designed to keep good principals on the job. As it is now, principals often have to move to a new district to get a substantial pay raise. In some cases, state rules need to be modified to allow local school boards to provide incentives for longevity and performance, but long-term contracts and sizeable resignation bonuses would help many of us get attached to our zip codes. Let's start paying principals to stay put!

The Principal as a Teacher

Another way for the high school principal to communicate a focus on teaching and learning is to be a teacher himself. When teachers see that the principal knows how to teach, relates well with students, and is comfortable in the classroom, that expertise creates almost instant credibility for the principal as an instructional leader.

There are various ways this can be done. My long-time colleague at Arapahoe High School, Ron Booth, frequently teaches individual lessons or units in classes throughout the school. I preferred to take on an entire teaching assignment from time to time, although not every year. In my years at Littleton High School, I taught a leadership course, an American Literature course, and the Theory of Knowledge course in our International Baccalaureate program. In addition, I taught several classes on a variety of topics to teachers in our school for which they received college credit. Students in my classes talk about their experiences with their fellow students and with their other teachers, and that publicity did me a world of good when it came to credibility with the faculty. The teachers who took my classes saw for themselves what I had to offer.

Being able to stand in front of the faculty and talk about where instruction in the building needs to go without anyone saying, or even thinking, "He (she) can't walk the talk" is a powerful arrow in the quiver of the principal who wants to be known as an instructional leader.

The Importance of Perseverance

Littleton High School has been recognized at local, state, and national levels for its high academic standards, its innovative programs, and its positive climate and culture. The National Association of Secondary School Principals (NASSP) recently included Littleton High School as one of only three high schools profiled in its seminal work on high school reform, *Breaking Ranks II: Strategies for Leading High School Reform* (2004). But there have also been setbacks and even failed attempts. In fact, that well-known line from a nationally televised sports program, "The thrill of victory and the agony of defeat," could be used to describe the history of school reform at Littleton High School. Examples of victories include the International Baccalaureate program, the program for at-risk freshmen, and the Senior-Year Plan. The continuing struggle to make a student advisement program work serves as an example of a "defeat." The important behavior to explore here is that of perseverance. An example from the past illustrates the point.

During the late 1980s and early 1990s, the Littleton High School community invested years of work creating a new system of schooling, the Direction 2000 program. The difficult task of converting requirements for graduation from seat time to performance-based requirements and all of the curricular, structural, and support changes that accompanied that move took thousands of hours and incredible amounts of emotional investment to complete. When the program was killed for political reasons in early 1994, the impact on the staff was devastating. In fact, teachers were seen weeping in the halls the day following the official school board action. For the remaining three months of that school year, teachers, for the most part, withdrew to the safety and security of their classrooms. They would work with their students, but they, understandably, were not interested in talking about large-scale school reform.

That could have been the end of school improvement efforts at Littleton High School, but it was not. Instead, the staff persevered in its pursuit of a system of education centered on clearly identified content and performance standards. If Direction 2000 was not to be allowed, how else could we accomplish our goals? By the fall of 1994, teachers were asking, "What are we going to do around here to get that Direction 2000 feeling of purpose and direction back?" The answer came in the form of essential tasks and the International Baccalaureate program.

During the 1994–95 school year, the faculty began to work on converting the Direction 2000 demonstrations (performance assessments) to essential tasks for which students would be held accountable at the course and department levels. It was not as powerful a system as Direction 2000 with its performance-based graduation requirements, but at least students would not be getting As and Bs in courses without having demonstrated mastery of a clearly identified set of essential learnings.

The International Baccalaureate program provided us with a set of internationally-recognized academic standards, standards that enabled our students to challenge themselves with the most rigorous program of secondary education available anywhere in the world. The faculty went back to that same board and received approval for the International Baccalaureate program in March, 1995, thirteen months after the crushing defeat of Direction 2000.

The virtue highlighted by this story is perseverance. The Littleton High School faculty persevered in their pursuit of an educational system based on clearly identified standards. That standards-based philosophy is alive and well at Littleton High School today. Longevity and perseverance are keys to lasting school improvement.

Balanced Authority in a Democratic Society

In his book, *The Red Pencil*, Ted Sizer (2004) asks us to think about who really "runs" our schools. His response to that question is informative to high school leaders who are trying to figure out who to involve in which decisions, and to what extent:

> My experience is that successful schools "run" on the basis of a series of understandings among the engaged partners, some of whom are close in, some removed. A principal explicitly or implicitly makes "treaties" with these various estates: the school's teachers and staff, the school's students, the students' parents or guardians, the customs and pressures from sister schools in the district and region, the district's central office, the community within which the school sits, the unions (whether formally organized or clusters of people who have a tradition of being heard), the district's school board, state authorities, federal authorities, local customs and expectations, associations (such as athletic conferences), external pressure groups and lobbies, the press, the school's "reputation"—not to mention immediate crises, such as budget shortfalls.
>
> School leaders I admire are those who have created a constructive balance of authority in their particular situations. They make "treaties," many of them unspoken, with the various estates. Those treaties are very local; a successful principal may arrange her affairs quite differently from another comparably successful principal down the street. The treaties are not primarily accepting of the status quo. Rather, they are treaties reflecting the central priorities of the school's leader, those embedded in the realities of the local situation, adapted as situations change and pressures wax and wane.
>
> Such "treaties" cannot be dismissed as nuisances. Rather, they are the stuff of democracy. Wise principals value them. Balanced authority—a crafting of shared responsibilities by means of "treaties"—is the heart of the American system. (pp. 33–34)

Sizer's notion of high school principals as treaty negotiators sheds important insight into the nature of leadership in one of the most complex organizations in American society. Organizational change research and theory more than suggest the involvement of key stakeholders in any and all school transformation initiatives. That involvement must include shared responsibilities—treaties, the stuff of democratic leadership in and for the high schools of our choice.

Notice, too, the adjective "balanced" used to qualify authority in the title of this section and in the quotation from Sizer. Democratic leadership does not mean that everything has to be put up for a vote. Sizer observes that the treaties negotiated by a principal reflect that particular school leader's priorities. Therein lies the balance, the common ground between the needs of the community and the values and beliefs of the person hired to lead that community. A very limited number of those values and beliefs, for each of us, are nonnegotiable.

Non-Negotiables

Have you read my book, *I'm Going To Be More Assertive If It's Alright With You?* Well, I really didn't write such a book, but I do think it is important for principals to be very clear, even assertive, about those things which are non-negotiable. Collaborative decision making is given so much attention today that principals are sometimes unnecessarily reluctant to announce their leadership prerogatives with an occasional "Now hear this!" As principal, I had some non-negotiables positions that, frankly, I wasn't really even interested in discussing with people—although I am always willing, even eager, to explain and support those positions. Using professional development time for teacher work time was a non-negotiable. "Spreading out the wealth" with regard to teacher assignments for both new teachers and veteran teachers was a non-negotiable. We would be an IB diploma school and not an IB certificate school. That was a non-negotiable. We would maintain an open-enrollment policy for our honors, AP, pre-IB, and IB courses. Remedial courses and tracts are bad for kids and need to be eliminated. I would make the final decision on all personnel matters. Personal professionalism, for example, being at work and in your classroom on time, returning phone calls promptly, and providing quality instruction from bell to bell was a non-negotiable. Being a continuous and a collaborative learner was not negotiable if you wanted to work at Littleton High School. It was okay if the word around the building on those and on a few other topics was "Don't even ask."

I have mentioned personal professionalism, but there is another aspect of professionalism that was also non-negotiable during my years at Littleton High School. Several years ago, two colleagues and I delivered a National Association of Secondary School Principals' professional development program to a large high school in Texas. The school has a solid reputation and is staffed with very talented individuals. The principal, who was relatively new at the time, is quite capable and very interested in school improvement efforts focusing on increasing student learning. Nevertheless, the other two presenters and I talk to this day about how unprofessional the faculty was during that workshop. In fact, we said then, and we still say now, "Thank

God that is not my school." I am sure we are being a little hard on that faculty, but what kind of first impression would you get from a group in which some individuals were reading the newspaper, grading papers, arriving late, leaving early, or, in a couple of cases, actually lying down on the floor at the back of the auditorium?

I had an opportunity to tell that story to my faculty not long ago when the question of professionalism came up in our school. A scheduling conflict took me away from the building during a half-day professional development day, something which happened for the first time in my twenty years at Littleton High School. When I returned, a half-dozen or so faculty members spoke to me about the "rude" and "unprofessional" behavior of a few of our colleagues. Side conversations, refusal to participate in activities, and intentionally obvious "packing up-ready-to-go" gestures were chief among the unprofessional behaviors listed. I spent a month or so speaking individually to teachers in order to get the benefit of their varied perspectives of what went on that day. When I felt I had a pretty complete picture, I addressed the faculty on the topic, not in a lecturing or scolding manner, but in a way that indicated, nonetheless, that the expectation of professional behavior at all times was non-negotiable. I told them the Texas story, and we all agreed that we did not want anyone to leave Littleton High School saying, "Thank God that is not my school."

Principals also need not be hesitant to exercise their leadership prerogative in making a command decision from time to time. Again, collaborative decision making is preferable as a general operating procedure, but I have seen organizations unnecessarily frozen by overanalysis and the expectation that everyone is going to be "involved." Some organizations are so analytical they're inert.

The usual procedure for hiring assistant principals at Littleton High School was to post the opening, allowing people from both inside and outside the organization to apply, and then to form a committee consisting of teachers, staff members, students, and parents to conduct interviews of a half-a-dozen or so candidates. The committee's charge was to send two candidates to the principal, both of whom they could be very excited about if chosen. I then made the final selection.

Recently, I made the command decision not to follow this process but to simply appoint a person to an assistant principalship. I will not bore you with all the details, but I decided that the timing of the opening, the demands of the position, and the experiences and qualities of the individual who was available to fill that opening rendered the normal selection process inappropriate. Instead, I appointed the person to the position and then sent a letter home (it was during the summer break) to each faculty and staff member explaining my decision and the rationale supporting it. I asked for neither permission nor forgiveness for my command decision. I also did not get any complaints. Sometimes, when the situation warrants the behavior, people appreciate it when "somebody just makes a decision."

Why be in charge if you can't have some non-negotiables and make some decisions?

Participation In Professional Development

Leadership for creating the high schools of our choice includes full participation by the principal in building professional development activities. As I have already mentioned, I have the opportunity to deliver professional development programs in high schools around the country, and I cannot tell you how many times I have seen the principal arrive late, be called out for messages, and/or leave early. What kind of message does this send to members of the faculty about the importance of professional development?

I do not teach writing, per se, but I participated fully in every single writing staff development training session or collaborative critical reflection session that we had in support of our writing power standard. I devoted my full attention to these sessions—no beeper, no cell phones, no interruptions for messages or to return phone calls. The same expectation applies to every member of my administrative team. The principal who commits herself completely to collaborative learning with the members of her faculty sends a strong message about what is important and communicates that she is more interested in being a leader than in being a manager.

You Are Who You Hire

Perhaps the most important thing I did as principal was to decide who worked at Littleton High School—who worked at Littleton High School as a teacher, who worked at Littleton High School as a clerical aide, who worked at Littleton High School as a coach. I had the final say on all personnel decisions.

When I hired teachers, I looked for people who were bright, articulate, energetic, passionate about their subject area, personally engaging, and fun. Oh, and of course, "highly qualified." I also looked for teacher candidates who asked good questions. I do not mean questions about salary and benefits, although that is okay at some point. What I was looking for were questions about educational philosophy, about our values and beliefs, about the kinds of relationships we want to foster among members of the education community and especially with our students, about my expectations for their performance, and about opportunities for professional growth. I was impressed with teacher candidates who wanted to, in one way or another, find out what kind of a place Littleton High School was. An engaging personality and a sense of humor are also important. If I did not find myself drawn into the conversation with a teacher candidate, I didn't hire that candidate. Someone without a good sense of humor simply would not have fit in to our faculty.

Early in my career, I was advised on more than one occasion to never accept someone for a teaching position that was not a "perfect match." In other words, never settle for someone who isn't everything you want because that person somehow has connections to the school community or can coach, or because it is late in the hiring season or the hiring pool is shallow. On one or two occasions over the last twenty-six years I have violated that principle, and I always regretted it. It is better to leave the position open or to fill it with a temporary assignment than to hire someone who you know from the get-go is never going to be a star. Jeff Bezos, Amazon.com CEO, says it well: "I'd rather interview 50 people and not hire anyone than hire the wrong person." (Deutschman, 2004, p. 55)

The same applies on the other side of the equation as well. Never keep a faculty member on the roster past the probationary period if you are not absolutely certain that he or she either is already or is going to be an outstanding teacher and faculty member. Again, I always regretted it when I hung on to someone past the probationary period because he did an "alright" job, or because he was "a nice guy," or because I thought he might eventually get better. It is better to start over, and over, and over again, if necessary, than to hang on to someone who is never going to be any more than just an "okay" performer.

Hiring the best teachers means to me hiring the best teachers in spite of building coaching and sponsorship needs. Members of the faculty, coaches, and parents knew I would not hire a good teacher who could coach over a great teacher who could not. That made it difficult on our athletic programs as we had a higher proportion of our coaches who came from outside the building than did most of our competitors. Nevertheless, it was another of those non-negotiables which I felt was essential to the accomplishment of our core academic mission. That position contributed to the development of what is arguably one of the finest high school faculties in the country. The connection between quality teaching and student achievement is well established by research.

The Role of Central Office and the Board of Education in Creating the High Schools of Our Choice

As Zmuda, Kuklis, and Kline (2004) have argued, "Context not only matters, but forms the crucial backdrop for any serious and enduring educational reform..." (p. vi). The Superintendent and other central office personnel, as well as the Board of Education, form a crucial context and backdrop for creating the high schools of our choice.

I was fortunate enough during most of my tenure at Littleton High School to work with superintendents and with school board members who valued site-based decision making, local initiative, and creative thinking, and who had the courage to challenge the status quo. It is perhaps this philosophy, more than anything else, of allowing decisions to be made closest to the student and allowing different sites to do things differently that contributed to our ability to accomplish the kinds of school improvements that we did at Littleton High School. Alan Bersin came to his job as superintendent of the San Diego Schools with that maxim clearly in mind:

> We emphasized the service dimension at the central office and underlined the fact that the role of the central office is to assist schools to improve instruction.... It's very important as we delegate more authority to school sites that the central office be turned into a service organization, serving schools, and headed up by people who maintain a constant focus on improving instruction. The key aim was to encourage [central office] people to invest in and support instructional decisions at schools. (Collaborative Communications Group, Inc., 2006, p. 7)

It takes courage on the part of the superintendent and a school board to have high schools with different graduation requirements, different athletic codes, different schedules, different philosophies, and different cultures as we did among the three comprehensive high schools in the Littleton Public Schools. Far fewer calls would come in from the public if everything were standardized across all schools. But that kind of thinking, although safe in the short run, denies the obvious differences among school communities, stifles creativity, and, in the long run, reduces choices for parents and students in the interest of making everything look the same. Superintendents and most school boards in Littleton have trusted principals and teachers to keep the best interests of students always in the forefront when making decisions regarding changes in the direction of our schools. I would not have remained as principal at Littleton High School for twenty years were that not the case.

Allowing, even encouraging, high schools to be different in their philosophies of education, learning theories, delivery methods, and organizational structures, while still holding them all accountable for achieving agreed-upon student achievement results, has become a popular position among high school reform advocates. The argument, one I have long supported, is that real choice is not available to students and parents if schools all look the same.

Two commissions on high school reform in Colorado recently issued recommendations supporting policies and practices, at both state and local levels, that encourage differences among high schools. The Colorado Commission for High School Improvement, a project of the Colorado Children's Campaign, issued a report in January 2005 that includes a principle on diversity of schools:

> Schools should be allowed to be different from one another. This principle encompasses both comprehensive high schools and specialized focus schools,

all with the purpose of helping all students learn to high standards and gain access to post-secondary education. We should create alternatives that serve Colorado's geographic diversity as well as options for independent and/or district-based, high-quality on-line education. (p. 6)

Similarly, a report in the *Rocky Mountain News* (2004) on preliminary recommendations from the Denver Public Schools' Commission on Secondary School Reform lists the following as "themes likely to appear in the final report":

♦ "Greater control at the local school level. Each high school would have more freedom in staffing, budget and curriculum but would be held accountable for results via performance contracts with the district.

♦ More choices in schools for students. Each high school would have a distinctive program such as a K–12 model or program for grades six through 12 or a school for English Language learners..." (p. 21A)

Reporter Allison Sherry of *The Denver Post* (2004) captures the shift in the Denver Public Schools from standardization to differences among schools in her coverage of that same preliminary report: "Tailoring curricula to the student, mentioned several times in the report, would be a departure from what DPS has worked several years to do: make every school's lesson plans uniform" (p. 15A).

Superintendents and boards of education in the Littleton Public Schools have always been very generous and supportive when it comes to administrators' professional growth. Our contracts provide for an adequate allocation to support attendance at conferences and workshops, and our supervisors have always been supportive with regard to participation in professional organizations, even though that participation requires us to be away from our buildings. The superintendent and his or her staff have been good models of continuous learning themselves, setting the tone for others in the district. In short, the Littleton Public Schools has a history of being an intellectually stimulating and nurturing place in which to work and grow. That kind of attitude from the superintendent and members of the board of education has untold benefits at the school and classroom levels.

Superintendents and/or members of boards of education who are dissatisfied with the pace of change in their high schools may do well to take a look in the mirror, for they provide the context and backdrop that either nurtures or is toxic to creating the high schools of our choice.

Part III

Personalizing Your School Environment

Chapter 5

Attitudes That Create High Schools Where Kids Want to Be

Personalizing the high school experience is a theme that dominates much of the literature related to creating high schools where kids want to be. A link between a personalized environment and high academic achievement is also beginning to be established. A report by the National Association of Secondary School Principals, *Breaking Ranks II*, contains a number of recommendations under the umbrella of personalizing the school environment and opens a major section of the report by affirming the link between a personalized environment and student achievement:

> If high achievement for all students is the goal of reform, then personalization and a rigorous curriculum are two essential ingredients. Although some students might be able to make it through four years of high school despite the lack of any personal connections, all students require a supportive environment—some more than others. Creating that environment is essential to bringing learning to fruition." (*Breaking Ranks II*, 2004, p. 67)

Ted Sizer, in his forward to *Breaking Ranks II*, confirms the necessity for personalization within the standardized framework:

> It is inconvenient that no two students are exactly alike and that no individual student stays exactly the same over his or her travel through the high school years. Batch processing does not work, at least for most adolescents. *Personalization* is a necessity if for no other reason than the fact that each individual student takes that state test, meets that required standard, performs in that demanded fashion, sinks that basket, sings that solo, writes that essay, solves that problem—one by one. A good school emerges from the creative weaving of distinctive parts into a whole cloth rather than from a

mindless assemblage of discreet programs, each protecting its independence. (*Breaking Ranks II*, 2004, p. xi)

Much, if not most, of the attention directed at high schools today focuses on academic achievement. Indeed, a section of this book is dedicated to the essential leadership function of creating a core academic mission in each high school. However, the high school experience should be about more than simply arriving at an academic-achievement "destination." Instead, the journey through high school itself ought to be enjoyable, rewarding, and fulfilling for students. Starbucks chairman and chief global strategist, Howard Schultz, understands that it is more than just the product that gets us to pay four dollars for a cup of coffee. What he is really persuading us to pay for is an ambience of relaxation and friendship. As he puts it, "We've known for a long time that Starbucks is more than just a wonderful cup of coffee. It's the experience." (Overholt, 2004, p. 53).

High School is more than just a framework for academic achievement: it's the experience. Futurist Gary Marx (2006) lists the following as one of sixteen trends that will have a profound impact on our future: "Standards and high-stakes tests will fuel a demand for personalization in an education system increasingly committed to lifelong human development" (p. 29). He further notes that "the outcome of the standards movement likely will be an increased demand for personalization of education. . . . Educators and public officials need to realize the only logical way to reach and exceed appropriate standards will be through personalization" (p. 30). Alan Bersin, California Secretary of Education and former superintendent of the San Diego City Schools, expressed a similar belief in a recent interview:

> We prepare our students for college and for the workplace. I think part of what we want to do with high school reform is to reinvent high schools to make them a very meaningful experience for academic and intellectual growth and social development on their own terms. . . . We need to stop devaluing high school by considering it merely as a stepping-stone to somewhere else. . . . high school ought [to] have significance on its own terms, in addition to serving as a bridge to higher education or the workplace. (Collaborative Communications Group, Inc., 2006, p. 5)

I have often said to entering freshmen, "This [high school] is the best time of your lives, so far." Such is not the case for too many of our high school youth. Commenting on the findings of a 2003 study by the National Research Council, Naomi Housman, Coordinator of the Washington-based National High School Alliance, concluded, "High schools have become a place where relationships are not strong. It's an alienating place for adults and kids" (Gehring, 2003, p. 5). *Breaking Ranks II* (2004) emphasizes the importance of strong relationships that contribute to personalization and thus to higher levels of academic achievement. Indeed, a strong argument can be made, and in fact has been made, for the position that the experience of high school should be as important a focus for high school leaders as is academic achievement. In other words, high school principals are responsible not only for gaining high levels of academic achievement for all students but also for creating high schools where all kids want to be.

In an article in *Kappan* entitled "A Balanced School Accountability Model: An Alternative to a High-Stakes Testing," Ken Jones argues that the physical and emotional well-being of students must be one of only five things for which schools should be held accountable:

> The caring aspect of school is essential to high-quality education. Parents expect that their children will be safe in schools and that adults in schools will tend to their affective as well as cognitive needs. In addition, we know that learning depends on a caring school climate that nurtures positive relationships. (Jones, 2004, p. 585)

Mr. Jones reaffirms what those of us in the business understand all too well— climate and culture, the experience of high school, matters.

Joseph DiMartino (2006), President of the Center for Secondary School Redesign at the Education Alliance at Brown University and a principal architect of *Breaking Ranks II*, identifies ten "basic tenets" of personalized learning:

- "Personalized schools promote the achievement of standards for each student.
- Personalized learning begins with individual interests so each student becomes engaged in learning.
- Teachers get to know each student's strengths, weaknesses, and interests.
- With school support over their high school experience, students become self-directed learners who can use learning to manage their lives.
- As students pursue an increasingly independent pathway, parents become true guides and mentors in the learning process.
- As students explore real options for their future in society outside of school, community members become involved in the schools in a meaningful way.
- Adults in the school model and benefit from stronger professional and student relationships.
- Against common standards, students learn to set goals and measure success for themselves.
- Students graduate upon demonstrating high performance in a variety of media, not simply high-stakes paper and pencil tests.
- Reaching all students depends on reaching each one." (pp. 5 and 11)

The authors of *Breaking Ranks II* (2004) talk about the importance of matching school relationships and practices to student needs for voice, belonging, choice, freedom, imagination, and success. (pp. 70–73) The publication contains recommendations for personalizing the school environment, which include breaking large high schools down into smaller, more personalized units; developing a Personal Plan for Progress for each student; assigning a personal adult advocate to each student; and flexible scheduling.

What possibilities await us here?

Trust and Responsibility

> "A community's functioning rests on trust..."
> (Sizer and Faust-Sizer, 1999, p. 17)

Creating high schools where kids want to be is all about creating relationships based on trust, as well as on responsibility and respect. In too many schools, students and adults get into an "us against them" game in which administrators and teachers expect students to be trying to pull something off and students do their best to accommodate those expectations. These environments are characterized by long lists of rules that attempt to codify every possible infraction that could incur and by tight supervision designed to catch students doing something wrong. Adults cannot win this game because in most schools there are fifteen or more potential perpetrators for every adult supervisor. To quote the Sizers again, "the rules that last come out of environments, not books." (Sizer and Faust-Sizer, 1999, p.17).

This "us against them" mentality is conspicuously absent in high schools with personalized environments. At Littleton High school, for example, adults assume that students are doing what they are supposed to be doing unless evidence clearly suggests otherwise. No one is assigned hall duty, and the only formal, assigned supervision is that two campus supervisors walk the parking lots and halls and, during heavy lunch periods, monitor the cafeteria. Littleton High School is an open campus for all students, and no one needs a pass to move from place to place in the building. Students can be seen walking in the halls, visiting with friends, sitting on the floor eating lunch, and engaging in various other academic and social activities during every period of the day. There are no study halls, and students can be anywhere in the universe they want to be during their unscheduled periods so long as they make it back to class on time. Students are trusted to do the right thing and are given a great deal of freedom and responsibility.

How do students respond? Graduation and average daily attendance rates at Littleton High School both exceed 95%, and fights and other disturbances are rare on the campus. If you expect people to do the right thing, most of them will, at least most of the time.

In *The Students Are Watching*, Ted Sizer and Nancy Faust-Sizer (1999) talk about student reactions to some of the negative messages sent by adults. For example, to the "suspicion and mistrust demonstrated by the security officer, festooned with a radio apparatus, patrolling a corner in the hallway, challenging kids as they hove into view," the students respond negatively themselves: "The kids laugh about him and his schtick, mocking him behind his back, but they've learned from his distressful stance, what their school thinks of them. 'They think we are dirt,' they tell us" (p. 12).

By trusting students and giving them responsibility, educators address their needs for freedom and choice. High schools where kids want to be are schools in which the message communicated to them from adults is not one of suspicion, but rather one of trust and respect.

Respect

In *Respect: An Exploration*, Sara Lawrence-Lightfoot (1999) defines respect as something much different from obedience or submission to a higher authority or compliance with dictates from "the top" (p. 9). In an online interview with David Gergen (*Online News Hour*, 1999), she further explains her definition of respect through the image of a circle:

> My view of respect is a circle. It is about symmetry. It's about reciprocity. Even if there are differences in knowledge and status and power and resources and skills, that respect is a great equalizer. It is the ways in which we are symmetric with one another, and it comes through this sense of connection in relationships. (p. 2)

In her book, Lawrence-Lightfoot asserts that this circle is based upon commitment and equality and says that respect consists of empathy, trust, and connection. Respect requires relationships developed over time and is best nurtured doing meaningful work together in the context of common values (pp. 9–10). Lawrence-Lightfoot outlines the important dimensions that create a framework for respect: they include empowerment, through which we allow others to take control of their own lives; dialogue, where we listen supportively to others; curiosity, the dimension in which we show a genuine interest in others, including an interest in knowing what they are thinking, feeling, and fearing; and attention, where we offer undiluted attention to others, sometimes in conversation and sometimes bearing silent witness (pp. 11–13). These components of respect align rather remarkably with the six student needs from *Breaking Ranks II* outlined earlier. It seems that we can meet most student needs and thus personalize education simply by treating students with respect.

Respect among all members of the school community, and particularly the respect that staff members model in their relationships with students, is essential to creating a positive experience for students in high schools. Sarcasm and "put-downs" are not messages of respect, whether used by adults or tolerated by adults when used by students. Those who honor diversity and divergent thinking do send messages of respect. Those who prefer anonymity—not knowing students' names or how to pronounce them correctly—do not express respect. But those who let students know who they are by sharing something personal and important do. Those who are late for class or for meetings do not show respect. Yet those who are organized and well prepared do. Those who use stereotypes or show favoritism do not communicate respect. Yet those with high expectations for all students supported by differentiated instruction and a school-wide support structures do. The implications of these and other messages of respect for school leaders are, I think, quite obvious.

The tragedy that struck Columbine High School on April 20, 1999, hit close to home for members of the Littleton High School community both literally and figuratively—literally because Columbine is only about five miles away and figuratively because the incident made us all realize just how vulnerable we are, wherever we live. Columbine was also a catalyst for a conversation at Littleton High School about what it means to have a culture of respect, a conversation that has had a lasting impact on the school.

That conversation has become a yearly event called "Coming Together in the Gym." On April 21st of each year Littleton High School students, faculty, and staff commemorate, not the tragedy itself, but what came out of it for the school. On the day after Columbine, we made the decision, rather spontaneously, to call everyone together in the gymnasium to talk about what had happened and to be together. We felt sad, confused, scared, and vulnerable. What happened there will remain forever in my mind as one of the most incredible testimonies to the human spirit that I have ever witnessed. For more than two hours students, and later faculty, stepped up to the microphone to talk about what it meant to be respected. Stories, tears, hugs, apologies, pleas, and commitments followed one after another until finally I had to adjourn the assembly to provide those in attendance with an opportunity to use the restrooms and get something to eat. It was a life-changing event for many of us.

Each year Littleton high School holds a "Coming Together in the Gym" assembly on April 21st to inform the new and remind the old members of the community of the commitment to respect that is part of the Littleton High School tradition. The message isn't that tragedy breeds respect, but rather that the failure of school leaders to seize opportunities to teach, model, and expect respect is always, in some respect, tragic.

In *The World is Flat*, Thomas L. Freidman, noting that India with its 150 million Muslims is the second largest Muslim country in the world, asks why there are no Indian Muslims in al-Qaede, no Indian Muslims in Guantanamo Bay, and no Indian Muslims fighting with jihadists in Iraq. The answer is, of course, complicated and multifaceted, but, in short, Freidman credits the democratic context in India that, unlike other more authoritarian Muslim countries, gives young people there a voice and a chance to succeed by working within the system rather than by blowing it up. His analysis of the impact of culture and context on behavior in the arena of world politics parallels, in a profound way, the effects of culture and context on the behavior of the young people in our high schools:

> Give young people a context where they can translate a positive imagination into reality, give them a context within which someone with a grievance can have it adjudicated in a court of law without having to bribe the judge with a goat, give them a context in which they can pursue an entrepreneurial idea and become the richest or the most creative or the most respected people in their own country, no matter what their background, give them a context in which any complaint or idea can be published in a newspaper, give them a context in which anyone can run for office—and guess what? They usually don't want to blow up the world. They usually want to be a part of it. (Friedman, 2005, pp. 458–9)

In reading that passage, I couldn't help but think: Give young people a school context where they can translate a positive imagination into reality, give them a context within which someone with a grievance can have it heard by his peers or by a respected adult without suspicion of favoritism, give them a context in which they can pursue an entrepreneurial idea and become the most creative or most respected people in their own school, no matter what their background, give them a context in which any Constitutionally-protected complaint or idea can be published in a newspaper, give them a context in which anyone can succeed-and guess what? They don't want to blow up the school. They want to be a part of it.

It's about respect, and respect is the key to personalizing education in our high schools.

"Getting to Know You, Getting to Know All About You . . ."

Teachers and principals who are interested in personalizing education and modeling respect would be well served by adopting that classic line from the Broadway musical, *My Fair Lady*, as a guiding principle. In a recent interview, Boston high school students identified making a serious effort to know every student well and creating opportunities for students to really get to know their classmates as among the top ways that teachers can improve a school climate (Boston Plan for Excellence, SY2004–2005, pp. 2–3). This call for personalization comes as no surprise, for each of us has, at times, experienced the heightened sense of worth that accompanies personalized recognition from someone whom we respect or who holds a position of authority.

Yet this common-sense principle seems to have been all but forgotten in many schools and classrooms. I am reminded of the time I observed a lesson in which students were expected to call upon a classmate to add to the responses they had offered. Although it was late in the semester, several students had to resort to identifying the next respondent physically by pointing or verbally with something along the lines of, "That dude in the second row," because they were unsure of their classmates' names. Or what about the school counselor or administrator at a recognition ceremony, or even graduation, who stumbles over the pronunciation of students' names? Does anyone in attendance believe from that point on that the school really knows (translates to "cares about") those students? Not a chance.

I once had an assistant principal who, in addition to being very visible in the halls and classrooms, had his wife use the yearbook to quiz him nightly until he knew the first and last names of every student in what was at the time a high school of about 1400 students. Students and parents marveled at how well he knew students (personalized education), and they often extended that conclusion to a judgment about the overall school environment. Counselors and administrators at Littleton high School sit down together before important public ceremonies to make sure of the pronunciation of students' names. And, of course, teachers who see themselves as teachers of students rather than teachers of content find ways of getting to know their students and of helping students get to know one another on an appropriately personal level early and often each term.

There are many variations on the "Getting to know you..." theme, but everyone in the high school who seeks to personalize education should be singing some easily recognizable version of that song.

"Good Morning"

Few things I did as principal contributed more to making Littleton High School a high school where kids wanted to be, and earned me more points with students, teachers, and parents, than did the high level of visibility I maintained in the halls, in the classrooms, and at extracurricular events during my twenty years as principal there. My greeting to students, staff, and parents when I saw them was a hearty "good morning," regardless of the time of day or night. This greeting became a trademark of sorts, and graduates often meet me with a hearty "good morning" when we run into each other years later.

The act of walking through classrooms has been explored for its contributions to teacher evaluation and principal visibility, and it has been identified as one of the most important influences on school effectiveness (Downy et al., 2004; Keller, 1998; Deal and Peterson, 1999). During my tenure, I tried to schedule a building "tour," lasting anywhere from two and one-half to three hours, at least three times each week. On those tours I had no particular destination, and I did not carry a cell phone or pager. At most, I informed my secretary of the general route I planned to take. I walked through classrooms and, when appropriate, asked students what they were doing and why. Students and teachers knew that a response such as "I don't know; we are just doing this because the teacher told us to" was the wrong answer. I also took time to visit with students in the halls and to stop by teachers' offices to visit socially, or, if initiated by the teacher, to engage in a discussion of school business. My tours usually included lunch with students in the cafeteria.

These classroom, hallway, and office tours were extremely valuable to me for many reasons. Students felt they knew me and were comfortable around me. Students and teachers felt that I cared about what was happening in classrooms. I got a sense of what was going on in classrooms, hallways, and common areas. Parents often remarked on how impressed they were when their sons and daughters said they had seen me in their classes during the day. And, just as important, my tours were the most enjoyable part of my day. If you enjoy watching good teachers do their work, and if you enjoy the vitality and energy of high school students, then you enjoy being out in the building.

The connections I gained and the relationships I established through these tours benefited me and, I hope, ultimately, the students beyond measure. Visibility facilitates communication too. I cannot tell you how many times each day a teacher or student would share an idea or concern with me for which they would never have scheduled an appointment. If I had only one piece of advice to give to a new high school principal, it might just be, "Visibility, visibility, keep yourself visible." (A companion contender is, "Delegate, delegate, delegate.")

I also attended more than my share of extracurricular events. Our administrative team divided up responsibilities for coverage of athletic events, concerts and plays, social events, and other school afternoon and evening functions. However, I often took more than my share. Such a commitment takes a toll on personal and family time, and each individual has to reconcile that in relation to his or her own specific situation. But professionally, I have never regretted the time I spent attending extracurricular activities and establishing relationships with students, coaches and sponsors, and parents. Frequently heard comments along the lines of "Dr. Westerberg, we see you at everything" were responsible in no small way for my longevity at Littleton High School. Attendance at extracurricular events helped me to establish relationships, to make connections, and to do my part to make our high school a place where kids wanted to be.

Schools in Which Kids Like Their Teachers

I sometimes hear teachers say, "They [students] don't have to like me; they just have to respect me." How about the old adage, "Don't let them see you smile until after Christmas"? Why do we continue to fill the heads of new teachers with such nonsense? Is it important for students to like their teachers? Absolutely! It is important, of course, to define just a little bit more clearly what is meant by the term *like*. I do not mean that it is important for teachers to be their students' "friends." Quite the contrary. Students do not need teachers to be their friends; they need teachers to be positive adult role models in their lives. In many cases, high school students spend more time with their teachers each day than they do with their parents. That time needs to be enjoyable, comfortable, and safe. Students should look forward to seeing their teachers each day, and teachers should look forward to seeing their students. Teachers should respect students and see them as not only being fun, but funny. High schools where kids want to be are schools in which students tell their parents from time to time, "I really like my teachers."

A personal story indicates how important it is to parents that their children like their teachers. I was at a restaurant one evening a few years ago when the parents of two Littleton High School students, one who had graduated and one who was a senior, came in and spotted me. I asked them to join me, and before long their conversation turned to how much their children loved Littleton High School. They listed many features during their flattering description of their son's and daughter's experiences, but at the top of their list was the fact that both kids "really liked their teachers." They were, in fact, so impressed with the teachers at Littleton High School that they rather spontaneously announced their desire to make a financial contribution to the school. About a month later they presented me with a check for $100,000.

The high schools of our choice must be schools with an attitude, an attitude that insists that each student's high school experience be one that is personal, meaningful, joyful—even intimate. In such a school, academic achievement is important, but it isn't all that's important. In such a school, students are known well by and like the adults who "control" and shape their lives. In high schools where personalization is a way of life and not just a slogan, students are seen as responsible young adults who are expected to do the right thing. Every high school student deserves to attend such a school, and you and I have a moral obligation to work to make that happen.

Chapter 6

Structures and Programs That Create High Schools Where Kids Want to Be

Personalizing education starts with an attitude, but is realized through institutional behaviors and commitments that "walk the talk." This chapter presents several structures and programs which help to personalize high schools. They include Block Scheduling, Freshman Academies, Student Advisement, Freshmen Transition Programs, Senior Transitions, and other programs and practices.

Block Scheduling

Block scheduling is a way to personalize instruction for students by giving schools the capability of adjusting time to meet individual student needs. Littleton High School moved to block scheduling in the mid-1990s to accommodate the needs of the school's standards-based constructivist learning theory. Standards-based constructivism is based on the premise that students must be given work to do—work that is tied directly to targeted standards for student performance—that allows them to construct personal meaning out of the information presented to them in school and elsewhere. By its very definition then, constructivism personalizes education for students.

A constructivist approach to teaching and learning focuses on big ideas. One of the gaps that exist between common sense and common practice in many high schools across the country is reflected in the attempt to teach big ideas in little snippets of time. Forty-six minute periods simply do not give teachers the time they need to implement a constructivist approach to teaching. The block schedule implemented at that time, and still in existence at Littleton High School today, is a modified block. All eight classes meet on Mondays (students typically take 6 or 7 classes and teachers teach 5). On Tuesdays and Thursdays, half of the classes meet for ninety minutes each, and the remaining classes meet for ninety minutes each on Wednesdays and Fridays.

More is said later about what constructivism looks like in the classroom. The point to be made here is that if there is any wisdom in the old adage that "form should follow function," then the way in which time is structured or formed in our high schools is important. If at least part of the function of schooling in the high schools of our choice is personalization, and if personalizing education involves making big ideas meaningful, then a master schedule that gives students time to delve deeply into concepts and bring closure to activities is an important part of a school's reform agenda.

The move to block scheduling at Littleton high School highlights two interesting observations, if not lessons, on the change process. The first lesson, for us at least, was that the move to the block had to be a complete move. For many years before our move to the block, Littleton High School had various schedules allowing either all classes or some classes to block one day each week. With few exceptions, those arrangements did not result in a change in instruction. In too many cases, teachers simply strung two lessons together, resulting in incredible boredom for students. Block days were the "unpopular" days under those one-day-a-week block arrangements, especially for students. Forty-six minute periods were the norm, and the one block each week was an uncomfortable deviation from that norm. Dabbling with block scheduling did not work.

Partly because of those experiences, the decision to move to a block schedule four days a week at Littleton High School was very controversial. In fact, the motion to do so was passed by our School Accountability Committee by one vote (six to five). Today, the block schedule at Littleton High School is strongly supported by the vast majority of teachers and students. I dare say that out of nearly one-hundred faculty members at Littleton High School, we would have trouble finding more than ten who would want to return to a traditional schedule.

What made the difference? When we went to a block schedule four days per week, teachers were forced to change their instructional strategies and to design lessons consistent with our constructivist learning theory; that is, they had to design lessons that actively engaged students in the construction of personal meaning. Of course, considerable staff development was provided to the faculty to facilitate this shift, especially during the first two years of transition and implementation. That change completely altered students' perceptions about the block. Of interest, now both students and faculty members are questioning why we have the "short" periods on Mondays, which, to many of them, seem too short to accomplish anything worthwhile and merely contribute to a school day that is fragmented and frantic. To make the block work we had to change the way that both students and teachers thought about classroom instruction.

The second "change lesson" in our move to the block schedule has to do with strategy. For a decade before our move to the block schedule the administrative team had been trying to interest the faculty in moving to a schedule that would result in fewer conflicts for students and that would better accommodate the aforementioned learning philosophy of the school. Throughout the years we had committees study at least a dozen variations of the major types of "flexible" schedules, but when decision time came the faculty always failed to muster enough support to move away from the present schedule. The existing schedule was the default schedule, and the default schedule always seemed to be the one the faculty members went back to when they began to feel uncomfortable with the uncertainties of change. The old saw—"People would rather live with a familiar pain than trade it for the uncertainties of an unknown pleasure"—accurately described our situation.

One fall we took a different approach. At our opening faculty meeting I announced that that year would be the last year on our present schedule. I supported my decision with data showing that many students had conflicts and suffered hardships under the existing schedule, conflicts and hardships that adults in the building would find completely unacceptable. The procedure I established made it clear that the decision on the following year's schedule would be left to our School Accountability Committee with significant input from the faculty, but that our present schedule would not be among the options on the list.

That move was tremendously liberating, and for the first time in a decade task forces in the building approached the assignment of looking at different schedules with the mind set that we would, indeed, select a new schedule for the following year. That strategy enabled us finally to move off of dead center on the scheduling issue, and it is a strategy that I have employed, selectively, at other times when I felt change in the operating structure of our school was a necessity. Empowerment does not mean never having to say, "no."

Freshman Academy

Like many comprehensive high schools across this country, Littleton High School has had a history of serving most students rather well while, at the same time, being frustrated with a lack of academic achievement on the part of others. Years of tracking grades at the school indicated that upwards of twenty percent of Freshmen and Sophomores received two or more Ds or Fs each semester, indicating to us that those students were not experiencing academic success. For years, our approach to dealing with those students not experiencing academic success was to have teachers and counselors work with them individually in the hopes of "motivating" them to be successful in our regular education program. We tried to change them to meet our system rather than changing the system to meet their needs. Those strategies worked with a few students, but not many, so we continued to experience a fifteen- to twenty-percent multiple "failure" rate each semester, year after year, decade after decade. Not very smart, is it?

Approximately six years ago we arrived at the conclusion that we had to provide some programmatic changes in order to reduce that multiple D and F percentage significantly, and we further decided that the greatest impact would be made by focusing on freshmen. The Empowerment Program was born in attempt to provide some intensive assistance for between twenty-five and thirty freshmen, primarily in literacy. That program operated with slight variations and with some success for five years. However, we were dissatisfied with the Empowerment Program on two fronts. First, the number of students served was well below the number in need of intensive assistance in order to experience success in the high school mainstream. Second, students in the Empowerment Program were doing reasonably well in that program but were continuing to fail courses taken outside the program.

The Freshman Academy Program was started in the fall of 2003 as a school within a school with the purpose of personalizing education for seventy high-risk ninth grade students while, at the same time, providing them with intensive assistance in literacy and mathematics. Four teachers were hired specifically to work in that program, two literacy specialists and two math specialists, and an assistant principal was assigned to function as the Freshman Academy principal as a part of his duties. The ninth grade counselor was assigned to work with the team as well. A section of the building was devoted to the program, and students were scheduled to spend five of their six classes in the Freshman Academy. The instructional time devoted to literacy and the instructional time devoted to mathematics were doubled in order to provide students intensive assistance in those two areas. The faculty believed that if students learn how to read, to write, to do mathematics, and, of course, to think well, they would be successful in their mainstream courses as sophomores. One period each day was set aside for social studies instruction. The indicators of success were increased student achievement scores in reading, writing, and mathematics and academic success in mainstream coursework at Littleton High School as sophomores.

To this day, the Freshman Academy Program provides personalized instruction for high-risk freshmen by providing a family-like atmosphere in which the students can work, by allowing students to have the same teachers all day, or nearly all day, by allowing significant relationships to be established, and by facilitating individualized instruction for students through lower teacher–pupil ratios. The benefits described in the literature on small schools and schools within schools with regard to personalization characterize the Freshman Academy Program.

It is important to distinguish between intensive assistance and academic tracking. The philosophy at Littleton High School is adamantly opposed to creating tracks for students in which they are exposed to low expectations and limited perspectives. Therefore, there will never be a Sophomore Academy, Junior Academy, or Senior Academy. The students in the Freshman Academy must improve their skills, study habits, and attitudes to a level where they can be successful in regular academic programs. The goal is to provide students with intensive assistance in literacy and math so that they can get out of the failure track and into a high school curriculum that prepares them for work and for further education.

Research from a recent study of three prominent high school reform models identifies freshman academies as a promising strategy for creating a personalized and orderly environment in American high schools (Quint, 2006, p. 20). The Talent Development High School model includes Ninth Grade Success Academies, which have been found to have positive effects on attendance rates, course credits earned, and rates of promotion to tenth grade (Olson, 2006, p. 24). Researchers at the Center for Social Organization of Schools at John Hopkins University, the University of Pennsylvania, and the Philadelphia Education Fund studying high-poverty, nonselective high schools found that one characteristic of schools that beat the odds and have high percentages of students who succeed at challenging coursework is "Strong instructional programs . . . matched with a schedule that allows for double-dosing in these [math and reading] subjects . . . ." (Balfanz and Legters, 2006, p. 42). Philadelphia is among the districts that provide double doses of math and language arts to freshmen who enter high school below grade level.

Proof of the Freshman Academy's success at Littleton High School, vis-à-vis the goals of the program, is just now becoming available as at the time of this writing the first group of Freshman Academy graduates had just finished the first semester of their sophomore year. Preliminary data, including retention rates, attendance rates, and first semester grades, are promising. At the end of the first semester of their sophomore year, fifty percent of the first Freshman Academy class had no failing grades, and another twenty-five percent had failed only one course. Those statistics are encouraging given that they describe a population of students who probably would have received multiple Fs had this special-needs small school not been created.

In schools in which large numbers of students are not experiencing academic success, conversion of the entire school into several small schools *with accompanying changes in teaching and learning at the classroom level* makes sense. However, there are communities in America in which many students are being served reasonably well by the comprehensive model and in which mustering the political will for whole-school change may be difficult. Under these circumstances, a school within a school for those students who need it might be the way to go. In either case, if the only arrow in your dealing-with-at-risk-students quiver is to change the kid rather than to change the system, you will probably end up shooting yourself in the foot.

A few words are in order here about the importance of changing what happens in the classroom when moving to the small-schools concept. Dividing a lousy, large high school into, let's say, four small schools without taking advantage of the opportunities that size, teaming, and the flexible use of time provide for creating relationships, developing professional learning communities, and changing the nature of teaching and learning results in little more than the creation of four lousy, small high schools. Largely because small schools have caught the attention of the Bill and Melinda Gate Foundation, and to a lesser extent the attention of the U.S. Department of Education, the small-schools concept has achieved "silver bullet" status in some school districts. Just convert existing high schools into small schools and student achievement will magically improve. After all, money talks.

However, reports prepared by the American Institutes for Research/SRI International and The National Evaluation of High School Transformation (AIR/SRI 2004, AIR/SRI 2005, *Executive Summary...*, 2005) on recent evaluations of the efforts of the Gates Foundation to improve student achievement by investing million of dollars in creating small schools revealed discouraging results, at least in math and particularly for existing schools. Among the implications cited in the reports is the importance of increasing the capacity of schools and districts to provide the staff development materials, offerings, and coaching needed by teachers to produce improved student outcomes in small-school settings. Kati Haycock, director of the Education Trust and one of the nation's most prominent advocates of closing the achievement gap between poor and minority children and their more affluent, white counterparts, recently commented that "When we look at the districts that are making the biggest gains, in terms of both overall achievement and narrowing gaps between groups, what seems to set them apart is their focus. They have very, very clear and high goals for kids. They focus a lot on instruction" (Borsuk, 2006, p. 2).

Again, research confirms the common-sense notion that school-improvement initiatives that leave teaching and learning in the classroom untouched will not yield increased student achievement. As Jane David and Larry Cuban (2006) concluded in their analysis of dozens of education reforms, "Simple answers and hoped-for miracles don't make a dent in the real world of schools and classrooms, except to fan disillusionment" (p. 110).

Student Advisement

Breaking Ranks II recommends that "every high school student have a personal adult advocate to help him or her personalize the educational experience" (NASSP, 2004, p. 85). Like most of the recommendations in that document, the creation of faculty advisory systems as a strategy for personalizing education is well supported by research. (Quint, 2006, p. 20; Boone, Hartzman, and Mero, 2006, p. 51) The notion that students need to make connections with their classmates, with significant adults, and with their community is not new to Littleton High School. Discussion of a student advisement program at Littleton High School began with a North Central Association study in 1988 that ultimately resulted in the restructuring of the school under a project entitled Direction 2000. In addition to a set of performance-based graduation requirements, Direction 2000 established a student advisement program, called the Educational Advisement Program (EAP), that began in the fall of 1991.

Littleton High School is now on its fourth iteration of an advisor/advisee program since the concept was introduced to students and staff in 1991. Because of rather significant changes in the Direction 2000 program brought about by political opposition to the program, the Educational Advisement Program was transformed in 1994 to the Personalized Education Program (PEP). PEP focused primarily on transitioning ninth grade students into the high school with upperclassmen attending sessions for registration and grade distribution purposes only. PEP was a weak program; consequently, the buy-in from students and teachers was weak as well.

In 1999, our School Accountability Committee adopted a proposal to create a program that would "support the Littleton Public Schools' mission statement and the Littleton High School vision statement by providing instruction and support for students to be successful in academics, interpersonal interactions, and transitions into, and within, the Littleton High School community." Thus was born the PRIDE program, which, once again, sought to provide a smooth transition to high school and from high school to the outside world for students, grades nine to twelve, by creating connections. Connections and relationships were the foci of the PRIDE program, and each member of the professional staff, including the principal, was a PRIDE advisor for a group of fifteen to twenty students grouped by grade level and gender. For four years, PRIDE groups met with their advisors for thirty-five minutes each Monday.

PRIDE, too, was controversial from the beginning, but we resolved to give the initiative four full years, one full cycle, before considering any significant changes in the program. Student, staff, and parent surveys were administered each year, and each year we found a significant number of people in each group who felt that the PRIDE program was not serving an important purpose.

A winter 2003 student survey indicated lukewarm support for the program, at best, with many students indicating, in a variety of ways, that the program had not made a significant difference in their four years at Littleton High School.

Our problem was that we lacked a clear academic purpose for our advisement program. During the original EAP days, advisors had a definite academic purpose because they were the ones who helped plan students' programs of study and who advised students and their parents on the collection of portfolio evidence needed to demonstrate mastery of our performance-based graduation requirements. Graduation from high school, quite literally, depended on the strength of the relationship between the advisor, the advisee, and the parents. With the loss of the Direction 2000 performance-based graduation requirements in 1994, student advisement at Littleton High School lost its academic purpose. The school community has struggled to recreate that purpose, and therefore a clear mission for advisement, ever since.

Many high schools in the country have gotten their purpose defined right and thus have created successful advisement programs. New Trier High School in Illinois, a suburban comprehensive high school of approximately 4,000 students on two campuses, has offered a successful student-advisement program since 1928. At New Trier, faculty advisors meet with approximately 25 students for 25 minutes each day. Advisors stay with their advisees for their entire high school experience, and advisee groups are organized by grade level and gender (e.g., tenth grade girls or twelfth grade boys). According to an online brochure, *The Adviser System*, "The adviser—along with the student's parents—helps the student plan an academic program suited to his or her ability and post-high school plans. The advisor also encourages and helps each student select co-curricular activities suited to individual interests."

Likewise, Waukesha North High School in Wisconsin, a suburban public high school that serves approximately 1,200 students, has found a way of building an academic connection point into its advisory program by incorporating ACT/SAT vocabulary building and applications of writing in the content areas into the advisement curriculum. Advisement groups meet every day for 30 minutes at Waukesha North, and, in addition to writing and vocabulary, the advisement curriculum emphasizes the Search Institute's 40 Developmental Assets, the Changing Lives Character Education curriculum, and community service. (Champeau, 2006, p. 25). James Madison High School in San Diego features advisory periods four days each week, with Tuesdays devoted to improving literacy, Wednesdays assigned to math skills, Thursdays focused on college preparation, and Fridays reserved for academic counseling. Advisory periods during the senior year are devoted to helping students prepare for the Senior Exhibition program. Again at James Madison we see a clear academic connection in the advisory program. (Boone, Hartzman, and Mero, 2006, p. 24)

The Met School in Providence, Rhode Island, is among several small schools, specialty schools, and charter schools that have made advisement an integral part of their school philosophies and programs. At The Met, a unique state-funded public school of around 350 students, "... all students belong to an advisory group in which a teacher-advisor guides the learning and development of roughly 14 students" (*Succeeding Together...*, 2005, pp. 1–2). Advisors help students create learning plans, find internships, and develop projects.

At the Francis W. Parker Charter Essential School in Devens, Massachusetts, all full-time teachers serve as advisors to twelve students or less and meet with those students for three hours each week. According to documents prepared by the school for presentation at the High School Showcase, advisories are intended to serve four specific purposes:

- *Academic Advising:* The advisory is a place to develop personal learning plans (PLPs), to monitor student progress in general and toward specific goals, to discuss teachers' assessments with students and parents, and to build upon the habits of learning.

- *Community Service:* The advisory is a place to practice being an active member of the broader community by designing and implementing community service projects.

- *Community Conversations:* the advisory is a vehicle for school-wide conversations about community issues, including school governance, and about being a community member.

- *Recreation:* The advisory is a place to have fun and to learn about group process and dynamics." ("Frances W. Parker Essential School...," 2005)

The members of The Francis W. Parker community are clear about the philosophy and purpose of student advisement. Notice too that the school's purpose statement begins with a clear academic purpose for the program.

A useful resource for high school leadership teams interested in creating student advisement programs, or in redesigning existing programs, has been created by the staff at The Francis W. Parker Charter Essential School (Figure 8). Entitled, "Six Key Dimensions of Successful Advisory Programs," the paper introduces the reader to important considerations with regard to purpose, organization, content, professional development and support, assessment, and leadership. The National Association of Secondary Schools' publication *The Personal Adult Advocate Program* is another good resource on developing and maintaining successful student advisement programs (Pope, Metha, and Webb, 1997)).

Much can be learned from schools that have built successful student advisory programs. The lesson learned from our years of creating and implementing high school advisor/advisee systems is that a definite academic purpose must exist for a full-blown, ninth- through twelfth-grade advisee system to be

Figure 8

SIX KEY DIMENSIONS OF SUCCESSFUL
ADVISORY PROGRAMS

Key Dimension #1: Purpose

Successful advisory programs have a clearly defined purpose or purposes that all members of the community understand and support and that all other key dimensions reinforce. There are many different purposes an advisory programs can be designed to meet, and therefore no two advisory programs will look alike. Each individual school must determine what it values and what it hopes to foster within its community. Listed below are some commonly stated purposes of advisory programs, each of which can foster personalization of a student's school experience.

- To advise students about academic decisions and monitor academic progress
- To provide developmental guidance (both formal and informal)
- To foster communication between the home and school and among members of the school community
- To encourage supportive peer relationships and practice conflict resolution
- To promote an awareness of diversity and tolerance
- To undertake community service both within and outside the school
- To facilitate community governance and conversations
- To prepare students for life transitions including career development, post-secondary opportunities
- To promote character development, explore moral dilemmas
- To explore the process of group development and have fun

Key Dimension #2: Organization

How an advisory program is structured has a significant impact on how personalized the advisory experience will be. Successful advisory programs organize themselves in ways that allow the stated purposes of the program to be met. In organizing/re-organizing the advisory program, three interlinked areas must be considered: people and size, time and space, and student ownership. (See organization questions to consider.)

Key Dimension #3: Advisory Program Content

The content of an advisory program will vary based on the purposes to be achieved, on the nature of the school, and on individual advisors, but is most successful when directly connected to students' academic, social and/or personal experiences. It may be organized around essential questions, themes, or skills. It may be consistent across advisories or vary based on an advisor's knowledge of his/her advisees. Advisors may follow a common curriculum,

(cont'd.)

Figure 8 *(Continued)*

SIX KEY DIMENSIONS OF SUCCESSFUL
ADVISORY PROGRAMS

pick and choose from an advisory handbook, or organize their own activities to personalize the advisory experience. Routines and protocols, that both advisor and advisees can count on to structure their experience together, are important.

Key Dimension #4: Professional Development and Support

Successful advisory programs are committed to providing initial advisory training and continuing professional development and support to advisors. Advisors who meet at regular intervals in various configurations (clusters, teams, full faculty, pairs) to discuss advisory issues feel more confident and experience greater success as advisors. Initial training and on-going support may include training in facilitation skills, the stages of group development, dealing with resistance and at-risk students, as well as structured time to have kid talk and to design/review curriculum.

Key Dimension #5: Assessment

Successful advisory programs are assessed at several levels to determine if the purposes of the program are being met, to determine if participants are meeting expectations, to measure other advisory program-specific outcomes, and to lend a seriousness and commitment to the program. These levels include: individual students/advisees; individual advisors; advisory groups as a whole; the overall advisory program; and the school and program leadership. The exact means of assessment will vary across schools as will the accountability mechanisms put in place. Assessment tools may include: simple checklists, interviews, surveys/questionnaires, advisory portfolios, observations, shadow studies, and various measures of school climate.

Key Dimension #6: Leadership

Successful advisory programs have strong leadership where an individual or team within the school community is charged with designing, implementing, overseeing, supporting, and assessing the program. Essential among the duties of the leadership are creating buy-in among community members and ensuring that advisors have adequate training, resources, and support. Proactive leadership is vital to avoiding or overcoming common barriers to successful program implementation.

Reprinted with permission of Francis W. Parker Charter Essential School and Sizer Teachers Center, Devens, MA.

successful. Too many high school teachers are not comfortable focusing on just affective education. However, with an academic purpose, the caring nature of most high school teachers enables the affective connections and re-lationships to develop as important by-products. Our opportunities became limited by our experiences; thus, we have been unsuccessful in re-establishing that academic–affective link in our advisor/advisee programs. Those experiences not withstanding, I continue to believe that the advisement concept is one worth investing in.

If I were to start anew in a school that did not have the experiences with advisement that Littleton High School now has, I would seek to engage the faculty in an advisor/advisee program wherein faculty advisors develop six-year plans (grades 8–13) with their advisees and help monitor and modify those plans throughout the high school experience. Some states are now requiring advisement programs intended to serve such purposes. Rhode Island requires all school improvement plans to provide a structure by which every student is assigned a responsible adult who is knowledgeable about the student and tracks his or her progress. Kentucky has a similar state-wide requirement, and South Carolina now requires schools to develop individual education plans for eighth graders with career planning beginning for all students in grade six.

Freshmen Transitions: The LINK Program

Contrary to what many of us "lifers" in high school education seem to think, life for our students neither begins nor ends in high school. In the spring of 2004, I recommended to the School Accountability Committee that the PRIDE program at Littleton High School be discontinued because of a lack of buy-in on the part of students and faculty. It has been replaced by transition programs for freshmen and seniors, with no formal advisement program in place for tenth- and eleventh-grade students.

The LINK program, a nationally recognized program, serves as a structure for our freshman transition program. Details about the LINK Crew program can be found elsewhere (www.boomerangproject.com or 1-800-688-7578). Basically, the program engages responsible junior and senior students in the mentoring of incoming freshmen through a very organized and quite well structured series of activities and meetings. Trained LINK advisors, volunteers from the faculty, work with the LINK leaders to ensure that the program is accomplishing its intended transition purposes. Although we "dabbled" with LINK for two or three years, the first year in which the full LINK Crew program was utilized in Littleton High School as the formal organizing structure for freshman orientation, induction, and transition was 2004–05. It is hoped that the program will provide a basis for the "personalization" needed to enable our ninth-grade students to feel a welcome part of the Littleton High School community.

Unedited testimonials (Figure 9) from both LINK leaders and freshman students at Littleton High School support the use of the LINK Crew program to transition students into the high school and thus personalize the high school experience.

Figure 9

LINK TESTIMONIALS

"You are fourteen years old and walk into a large foreign building. No one in this building is familiar. Do these foreign creatures even speak the same language? Suddenly you spot the bright shirt of a LINK leader and you know everything will be okay.

A week before this terrifying day, the freshmen met and socialized with their peers and upperclassmen (LINK leaders). Throughout this day we (the LINK leaders) helped build a strong bridge for each individual from middle school to high school. This day was Freshman Orientation; new friendships were created, and we assured each freshman that they were just as important as any upperclassman. By the end of this day the freshmen gained more self confidence and much of their stress was alleviated.

We wanted to participate in LINK because it is a very strong program and we have always heard positive feedback about it. Furthermore, we had a blast during our Freshman Orientation and remember how great we felt when the day was over. By joining LINK we knew that we could make a difference within the school community by creating a positive and comforting atmosphere. We have built strong relationships with our freshmen. We hope they will desire to further the success of the LINK program in years to come!"

Courtney and Helen
Juniors at LHS

"As a LINK leader I have learned many things and benefited greatly from the experience. The LINK program at Littleton High School is in my opinion, still developing. There are many ways in which the program can be improved, primarily the communication between the link leaders and the freshmen. When freshmen are new to Littleton High School, they feel as if they know everything. Advice that is given to them by the leaders should be taken more seriously. I feel that it is extremely hard to get in touch with the freshmen when they are not as accepting as one would hope. Freshmen tend to take on a defensive attitude, instead of just accepting help and guidance. Overall, the LINK program will in the future have a positive effect on the environment of our school. Because of the LINK program, I have noticed that freshmen feel more "at home." When students feel comfortable in their environment, they most likely will have success in their academics as well as the social aspect of high school."

April
Junior at LHS

"I think that LINK was a good way to get connected into the social pipeline. It got me started out more comfortably. Knowing kids and being able to say 'hey'

(cont'd.)

Figure 9 *(Continued)*

LINK TESTIMONIALS

---

to them was pretty cool. Some of the kids that I met in my LINK group and I are still pretty good friends. Overall, LINK was great and got me started off on the right track."

Ethan
Freshman at LHS

"What I think about LINK is that it is a good thing to have. I think this because it helped me and a few other people I know get help with tutors and other things like studying tips. I personally think that they should keep doing it so that the 9th graders get help with anything having to do with school."

Brandon
Freshman at LHS

"I think that LINK is an idea that can improve someone's time here at Littleton. Why? Because it can inspire some of the kids that go here to try a little harder. But I don't think that many kids know that LINK is helping them out. The things that helped me out were how to prepare for the mid-term exam and to manage my time so I'm not overloaded. I think that LINK made everyone feel a little more comfortable, because everyone is a little afraid of something new. It was nice to have an idea of what was coming and the best way to enjoy it."

Hannah
Freshman at LHS

The transition piece for seniors comes in the form of the Senior Year-Plan, which is the subject to which we now turn.

Senior Transitions: The Senior-Year Plan

A federal commission recently singled out the senior year in American high schools as an academic wasteland (*The Lost Opportunity of Senior Year . . .*, 2001). That commission is not alone. Other reports over the last five years have identified the senior year as ripe for rethinking. (Raising Our Sights . . . , 2001; Kirst, 2001.)

At Littleton High School we have been forever painfully aware of the dreaded "senior slump," especially the second-semester senior slump. By the time second semester rolls around, many seniors have met all or nearly all of the requirements for graduation and have been accepted into college. A few students are held in place by upcoming Advanced Placement and International

Baccalaureate exams, but they represent only about twenty-five percent of the students in each senior class in a school that sends ninety percent of its graduating seniors off to college. A look at the Littleton High School class of 2002 reveals that over half (53%) of the students in that class already had enough credits to graduate by the end of the first semester. Many more needed only one or two courses to complete the requirements. For too many students, then, the second semester is one of "filling up the schedule," preferably with "easy" classes. Students are poorly motivated when forced to take classes they do not need or want just to be fully scheduled. Teachers report a lack of motivation and even the presence of disruptive behavior by students who simply do not want to be, and perhaps should not be, in some of their scheduled classes.

The Senior-Year Plan is an example of a personal plan for progress developed for the purpose of personalizing education as recommended by *Breaking Ranks II* (2004). Littleton High School hopes to make the second semester of the senior year more of a transition to life after high school by engaging students in coursework and experiences that provide a direct link to what they plan to do after high school. In addition to coursework at Littleton High School, options include coenrollments at local community colleges and universities, internships, independent studies, community service work, distance learning, travel, and capstone or research projects. During the second semester of their junior year, students are asked to develop a reflection piece, thinking back on their high school experiences thus far. During the first semester of the senior year, seniors work with their advisors to develop a plan for the second semester. The senior year time line is illustrated in Figure 10.

Students participating in any type of alternative programming (that is, something other than a full schedule of courses at Littleton High School) must complete an application that has to be signed by the student, the advisor, the parent, the counselor, and an assistant principal. Experiential learning activities (internships, for example) are monitored through communication between the advisor and the person in the community sponsoring the experience.

During the second semester of the 2002–03 school year, sixty-six seniors—twenty percent of the senior class—took one-hundred and fifty courses, totaling four hundred and fifty credits at a local community college. All but a few of those students were concurrently enrolled in coursework at Littleton High School. During that same year, fifty-three students included an internship or some other form of work experience in their Senior-Year Plans. These students were also coenrolled in courses at Littleton High School while learning to be dancers, photographers, coroners, automotive technicians, certified public accountants, interior designers, firefighters, culinary artists, physical therapists, public defenders, and real estate agents.

The experience of one of my advisees from the Class of 2003, Reese, serves as an example of how the Senior-Year Plan can benefit students. Reese planned to attend Colorado State University after graduation from high

Figure 10

SENIOR-YEAR TIMELINE

January–May

- ◆ 11th grade PRIDE meets as a group to communicate timeline
- ◆ Juniors conduct credit checks to ensure graduation requirements are met
- ◆ Juniors begin reflection piece of senior plan
- ◆ Reflection pieces due to PRIDE advisor by the last PRIDE session of the school year
- ◆ Post-Secondary Options Act applications turned in by May 1

August–November

- ◆ 12th grade PRIDE meets as a group to begin organizing second semester plans
- ◆ 12th grade PRIDE advisors meet with individuals during PRIDE to check on progress of second semester senior plan
- ◆ 12th grade PRIDE advisors distribute six-week grades
- ◆ Seniors with plans containing experiential activities turn in draft of plan to PRIDE advisor by November 1
- ◆ Seniors with plans containing traditional coursework and activities turn in complete and signed plans to PRIDE advisor by November 1

Senior Plan Approval Committee
- ◆ Parent/guardian
- ◆ PRIDE advisor
- ◆ Community member (if applicable)

December

- ◆ Seniors with plans containing experiential activities present plans to committee for approval by December 1
- ◆ ALL senior plans complete and signed by finals week

January–April

- ◆ Seniors implement second semester plans. PRIDE advisors monitor and advise individual seniors

May

- ◆ PRIDE meets as a group over several weeks to share experiences and conclude Final Thoughts
- ◆ GRADUATION!!

school and earn a degree in business. His career goal was to be in real estate. Reese's plan for second semester of his senior year included taking two courses at Littleton High School, taking two courses related to real estate at our local community college, and serving as an intern at a local real estate agency. Reese successfully completed his senior-year plan and considered the second semester of his senior year the most productive of his high school experience.

The Senior-Year Plan at Littleton High School is designed, in the words of one national report, to make the senior year more like a launching pad than a rest stop. (*Raising Our Sights . . .*, 2001, p. 11). During the students' senior year at Littleton High School, they have one foot planted firmly in the coursework and environment of our high school while, at the same time, stepping out into their futures with the other foot.

Challenging Coursework

High schools where students want to be are schools where the coursework in which students are engaged is considered to be challenging, intellectually stimulating, and meaningful to the students themselves. Much has been written recently, however, suggesting that this is not the case for too many high school students in this country. "High Schools of the Millennium," a report issued by the American Youth Policy Forum in August 2000, has the following to say about what high school students in this country think about what they are doing in their classrooms: "Today's students feel as though high school is irrelevant, the classes are boring, and that they are just passing time until something important, like college or a career, comes to pass" (p. iv). Reading the literature on student attitudes toward school, Pedro A. Noguera of New York University concludes that "pervasive student alienation, boredom, strained relationships between adults and students, and anti-intellectual peer cultures undermine efforts to raise student achievement." (Noguera, 2004, p. 26). In *Education Week* (December 2003), The National Research Council reports similar sentiments on the part of high school students toward what they are learning and doing in the classroom.

The negative statistics are overwhelming because of their sheer numbers. McCarthy and Kuh (2006) discuss a survey of more than 170,000 students in grades 9 through 12 in 167 schools across 28 states conducted by the High School Survey of Student Engagement in 2005, which found that only 51% said they were challenged to do their best work at school, less than half said their schoolwork makes them curious to learn about other things, and just over a third were excited about their classes (p. 666). Bridgeland, Dilulio, and Burke Morison (2006) point to the statistics garnered by Civic Enterprises in 2006 from a series of focus groups and a survey of 16–25 year olds who identified themselves as high school dropouts: "...47 percent said a major reason for dropping out was that classes were not interesting...; 69 percent said they were not motivated or inspired to work hard; 80 percent did one hour or less of homework each day in high school; [and] two-thirds would have worked harder if more was demanded of them" (p. iii).

It is obvious that many high schools in this country need to re-examine the work that students are being asked to do if we are to make our high schools places where students are intellectually stimulated—that is, high schools where kids want to be. As Gehring (2003) has argued, members of the education community should "think more creatively about how school settings and instruction can be tailored to address that sense of alienation... what's important is really making sure both the academic rigor is solid and the relationships are there at many levels" (p. 5)

Littleton High School acted on two specific fronts over several years to help ensure that the school is an intellectually stimulating place to be for all students. Those two "fronts"—the elimination of remedial courses and open enrollment for college-prep and college courses for all students—are the result of both philosophical and structural changes in the school.

Twenty years ago, Littleton High School had remedial tracks in all core subject areas. They were called "basic skills" courses. Life in those remedial courses, for both teachers and students, was a nightmare. The content was watered down, the instructional strategies were largely "formulaic," the expectations were low, and absenteeism and incidents of disruptive behavior were high. What's more, few students ever got "remediated." Students in basic skills ninth-grade language arts, for example, were also in basic skills tenth-grade language arts, basic skills eleventh-grade language arts, and basic skills twelfth-grade language arts, and they still could not read or write. Similar patterns existed in math, science, and social studies. Today, there are no remedial courses offered at Littleton High School. For example, the mathematics department offers courses only at the level of algebra and above.

Educators and parents sometimes worry that failure and dropout rates will go up with the elimination of remedial coursework. That simply has not happened at Littleton High School. In fact, the failure and dropout rates are lower now than they were twenty years ago, although those accomplishments are, no doubt, the result of many different initiatives at the school. Additional weekly lab periods are scheduled in some disciplines so that students who have been identified as being at risk can get the assistance they need to be successful.

Janice I. Somerville of the National Association of Assistant Heads and the Education Trust, speaking at the forty-fourth ACT annual meeting, recently proclaimed, "Remediation is like the canary in the mine shaft—it tells us big, bad things are happening" (2004, p. 10). In my opinion, and in the opinion of many others, remedial coursework in America's high schools has to go.

The other side of that coin is an open-enrollment policy that encourages all students to try college-prep and college-credit classes. In 2003, Littleton High School was listed by Jay Matthews of the *Washington Post* as one of the top high schools in America based on the number of Advanced Placement and International Baccalaureate tests taken as a proportion of the number of students in the senior class (p. 8). That happened, in part, because of the philosophy at Littleton High School that offers enrollment in honors, pre-IB, Advanced Placement, and International Baccalaureate courses and programs to anyone who is willing to take on the challenge and has even a slight chance of being successful. The only thing a student has to do to qualify for Advanced Placement English, for example, is to sign up.

There are schools that limit the number of students who can be in such courses through rigorous, and often artificial, placement criteria (e.g., standardized test scores and GPAs) and/or through quotas on the number of students in each cohort group who will be allowed to enroll in high-level classes. It is little wonder, then, that the National Center for Education Statistics reported "that 28 percent of all entering freshmen nationwide in 2000 needed at least one remedial course." (Hupfeld, 2006, p. 10). That is not the direction where we should be headed if our goal is to create schools in which students find personal meaning. By way of contrast, a common feature of NASSP's Breakthrough High Schools (2006) is the expectation that all students participate in challenging college preparatory coursework (p. 51).

The creation of high schools where kids want to be has a lot to do with the academic challenge and intellectual interest of the coursework in which students are enrolled, and the elimination of remedial classes and opening up of enrollment for academically challenging courses are important steps in pursuit of this quest.

Constructivism as a Learning Theory

> "Teachers will design high-quality work and teach in ways that engage students, encourage them to persist, and, when the work is successfully completed, result in student satisfaction and their acquisition of knowledge, critical thinking, and problem-solving skills, and other abilities valued by society."
>
> (*Breaking Ranks II*, 2004, p. 126)

Kids want to be in schools where what they are learning has personal meaning. Several years ago, in response to the research from cognitive psychology about how people learn and to the emerging applications of brain research to education, Littleton High School adopted standards-based constructivism as a guiding learning theory. What this learning theory means in practice is that teachers must develop work for students that causes them to construct personal meaning out of the knowledge and information presented and available to them. If education is nothing more than repeating what the teacher or the textbook says the meaning of something is, then it is a pretty dull experience indeed and will probably result in little more than end-of-the-unit data dumps. Sometimes those data dumps take the form of students literally dumping the contents of their notebooks in the trash following a unit or semester exam. More often, it is less visible but more discouraging in the form of an attitude on the part of students who say, "I don't have to know that anymore; the test is over," which is essentially a mental data dump. Such an attitude tells us that the unit content and skills were meaningful only to the teacher. All that had meaning for the students was playing the school game and getting the grades they wanted. Surely we want more return for our investment than that.

The qualifier—"standards-based"—is important in distinguishing what we do from its more common but coherence-challenged cousin, "activities-based constructivism." The work teachers design for students to do, those concepts and skills for which we want them to develop some personal meaning, must be tied directly to building, district, and state standards. Personally meaningful activities which are not anchored in the curriculum are a luxury we cannot afford. Instruction in a constructivist classroom actively engages students in designing, presenting, evaluating, analyzing, demonstrating, explaining, and applying—active verbals—the meaning of content and skills contained in relevant content standards.

Assessment looks different too in a standards-based constructivist school. Instead of just regurgitating back what the teacher or the textbook said, students actually must do something to demonstrate a personal (personalized) understanding of essential learnings. With a constructivist approach to assessment, teachers and students need rubrics, not scoring keys. The next five figures (Figures 11–15) describe and illustrate what assessments designed to accommodate Littleton High School's standards-based constructivist philosophy should look like.

High schools where kids want to be are schools in which learning is personally meaningful.

Figure 11

MEMORANDUM

DATE: January 21, 2003
TO: All Members of the Faculty
FROM: T.W.
SUBJECT: Final Exams

If you have not already done so, now is the time to think about your final exams for this semester. Introducing the semester by describing for students the kind of performance that will be expected of them at the end provides a destination for the arduous learning journey they are being asked to begin. Focus, direction, and context are essential to motivation, meaning, and purpose.

With that in mind, I would like to share a few of my thoughts with you regarding final exams.

It is important that you think about your philosophy and the purpose of final exams in your courses. For example, do you believe that the primary purpose of a final exam is to serve as a review of the content and skills uncovered throughout the semester in the hopes that one more "run through" of class notes and textbook materials will insure long-term retention? Do you believe that the purpose of final exams is to give students a chance to boost their grades? In either case, do research and your own experiences support these beliefs?

My own view is that the final exam should be a *culminating* experience that asks each student to bring *personal meaning* to *essential* course learnings. The final exam is not a recapitulation of the "parts" of a course. It is, instead, an opportunity for the student to put the parts together in a personally meaningful "whole." The whole is, indeed, more than a sum of the parts!

If you subscribe to this philosophy a final exam that consists mostly of test questions from previous unit tests is probably inappropriate. If you subscribe to this philosophy your exams focus on student answers to course essential questions rather than student regurgitation of predetermined "expert" answers. If you subscribe to this philosophy you have a scoring rubric but no answer key as bringing personal meaning to knowledge means that each student's response will be unique. If you subscribe to this philosophy you view the final exam as more of a learning than an evaluative tool. The research is pretty clear—learning is not retained sans personal meaning. What are you telling students about the performances that will be expected of them in May? Whose "answers" will be on the final exams you give, yours' or your students'? Whose final exams are they? Will students be given an opportunity to demonstrate "the whole thing," or are the words of the commercial slogan from the '80s words to live by in the case of final exams—"parts is parts?"

Think about it.

Figure 12

PHYSICS 2001
Final Assessment

For the past ten months you have been introduced to a wide range of concepts, facts, and skills considered important in understanding the science discipline of physics. It is now time for you to construct meaning to what you have learned. You now have the opportunity to think and write about what you believe are the essential things you have learned in this course. To assist (and assess) you in this task, I want to tell you a story!

The story is about Janus, the Roman god of beginnings and endings. Janus was the ruler of Latium (present-day Italy) and brought his people a golden age of peace and welfare. He introduced money, the cultivation of fields, and just laws for all members of Roman society. After his death, he was worshiped at the beginning of harvest, marriage, and other important times in an individual's life. The beginning of a new year in the Roman calendar, January, is named for him. Janus also came to represent the transition from adolescence to adulthood and is represented with two faces, one looking to the past, the other looking toward the future (*Encyclopedia Mythica*, 1999).

(Image courtesy of Kyle Pope, Ancient Road Publications, http://kmpope.home.att.net)

Your final assessment is to, within the context of physics, and like Janus, look back while looking forward toward the future. Carefully read the following requirements and use the rubric on the back to complete your task.

1. You must create a "stained glass" depicting your study of physics. The "stained glass" will be a *hand-drawn*, *colored set* of six panels placed together on a 2' x 3' poster board. You must provide all the materials necessary to complete your final product.

2. Three of the panels must represent topics, facts or skills we have studied that are most important to you. The topics may be important to you personally or because they helped you organize or understand science or because of the effect they have on society in general. Each of these three "past" panels should be lifted up to reveal a word-processed brief, which accurately describes the topic/fact/skill and reveals to the readers its importance to you.

3. Three of the panels must represent *different* topics, facts, or skills we have studied that you feel are important to the future. They may be important to you personally or to society in general. Each of these panels should lift to

(cont'd.)

Figure 12 *(Continued)*

PHYSICS 2001
Final Assessment

---

reveal a word-processed brief, which accurately *and* reasonably tells the reader how these are important to the future. You must document each of your predictions with a reputable source.

4. Research and word-processing *may be* conducted outside of class, but drawing and construction of the final product must be done in class. Senior finals will be collected at the end of the block on Friday, May 18th. Underclasspersons' assessments will be collected at the end of their scheduled final. The penalty for early *or* late completion is real and severe.

Figure 13

"IS NATURE BALANCED?"
Field Stream Study 2001

"Is nature balanced?" has been our guiding question throughout the whole year. Now, you have the chance to relate your findings at Big Dry Creek to this question. This activity is the culmination of a year's worth of work, as well as a celebration of knowledge that you have learned in Integrated Science for the past two years.

Even though your research in the field continues, it will be important to consider the following questions:

Is balance in nature important?
What is a healthy ecosystem?
Is balance necessary for a healthy ecosystem?
What evidence is need to determine a healthy ecosystem?

As you study the ecosystem at Big Dry Creek, you will be using a varied range of observations to help you address the above questions. Each member of the team will lead the group through a series of procedures that will help with the conclusions you draw regarding the questions above.

Organization and cooperation is critical if your team is going to complete this project successfully and produce a stellar presentation. Each member of the team will, at some time, be the leader of the group. Leadership skills are critical at these times; however, you will also be required to follow instructions given by another. Remember, the final goal is to answer the question "Is nature balanced?" with a significant body of supporting evidence. Achieving this goal will require that each member of the team works to support all individuals.

(cont'd.)

Figure 13 *(Continued)*

"IS NATURE BALANCED?"
Field Stream Study 2001)

The final product of your group will include the following:

♦ an oral presentation (10 minutes in length) to the class answering the question "Is nature balanced?" as well as predicting HOW the state of the stream may change due to a given impact

♦ (information on the impact will be given at a later date)

♦ two posters that display: two detailed maps (one overhead and one profile), data on biotic factors both land and aquatic, microclimate data, soil data, and stream data (specifics of this data are in individual packets and on the final rubric)

♦ analysis of how each category of data contributes to the final statement on the balance of nature

Each member of the group is expected to contribute to the final presentation by

♦ explaining how data in his/her *specific* area contributed to the final statement of the group and

♦ making sure that his/her data are complete, accurate, and informative on the final posters

Your grade for the stream study and presentation will be your final grade in this class. It will be based on the following:

♦ successful completion of your portion of the study (data collections sheets)

♦ ability to work effectively with group members (as leader AND as supporter)

♦ overall poster

♦ final presentation

Figure 14

ESL SOCIAL STUDIES FINAL PROJECT: DESIGN YOUR OWN GOVERNMENT
due Friday, May 18th
200 points

For your final project, you will design your own, ideal government. You will use the information that you have learned this semester about the US government and your ideas on how to improve what we have. You must thoroughly explain what your government will look like, what will stay the same, and what will change from our current U.S. government. You must include at least 10 changes for each branch of the U.S. government—executive, legislative, and judicial.

Your description of your new government must be very *specific* and it must answer *why* and *how*.

Please begin by writing down at least 10 ideas for changes (below), then approximately 10 concepts that will stay the same (on the back of this paper). After doing this, run these by me for my approval/suggestions.

You will present some (not all!) of your ideas for changes on May 18th, so please be prepared to do so.

Part 1—What will change? How is this a change?

U.S. FEDERAL GOVERNMENT

Legislative	Judicial	Executive
1.	1.	1.
2.	2.	2.
3.	3.	3.
4.	4.	4.
5.	5.	5.
6.	6.	6.
7.	7.	7.
8.	8.	8.
9.	9.	9.
10.	10.	10.

Figure 15

SCREENWRITING/VP
Final Exam

Consider the documentary "Hearts of Darkness: A Filmmaker's Apocalypse."

Compare and contrast your own movie-making experience to the experience detailed in the movie. Then connect your experience to the concepts of effective screenwriting—CZ, true character, conflict (internal and external), flaw, obstacles/tasks, and climax. Be creative and interesting!!!

Finally, offer any suggestions for course improvements:

- What should stay as is?
- What should be modified?
- What should be scrapped?

Part IV

Curriculum, Instruction, and Assessment

Chapter 7

Creating High Schools with a Core Academic Mission

The driving force behind a school vision statement is a core academic mission. In *The Students Are Watching*, Ted Sizer and Nancy Faust-Sizer write, "High schools have long had three core tasks: to prepare young people for the world of work; to prepare them to use their minds well, to think deeply and in an informed way; and to prepare them to be thoughtful citizens and decent human beings" (1999, p.10)

In a keynote speech at the CASE High School Summit in 2004, Tom Vander Ark of the Bill and Melinda Gates Foundation identified the development of "a single unifying mission for your work in your school" as the first step in any significant school improvement campaign. He suggested beginning the development of that mission through conversations about the purpose of your high school and the purpose of education. Mr. Vander Ark then suggested what that mission ought to be:

- ♦ To make all students ready for college, work, and citizenship;
- ♦ To ensure that all students are prepared to participate in further learning (post-secondary success); and
- ♦ To help all students leave high school with a sense of direction.

Breaking Ranks II has a great deal to say about the mission of the twenty-first century high school, which can be summarized as containing two primary components:

- ♦ To engage every student in a rigorous, relevant, coherent course of study that prepares him or her for college, work, and citizenship; and
- ♦ To ensure that every student is educated in a respectful, personalized, and supportive environment. (NASSP, 2004)

Rigor, relevance, and relationships are what high schools are all about according to the *Breaking Ranks II* commission.

Mission statements that are longer than a sentence or two usually do not say anything. The Prego approach to mission writing ("It's in there!") sacrifices clarity and functionality to the temptation to accommodate everyone's pet purpose. In this regard, Noble High School in North Berwick, Maine, has it right: "Every student college ready without remediation." That phrase sums up the mission with simple, clear, and discriminating brevity. The mission statement of the School for Human Rights in New York City communicates clearly and directly what the school is all about: To produce "socially engaged young adults committed to equity, dignity and social consciousness." And what Thomas Friedman, author of *The World is Flat*, calls a vision statement might serve some high schools as a mission statement: "JFK wanted to put a man on the moon. My vision is to put every American man or women on a [college] campus" (Friedman, 2005, p. 290).

A Bloated and Fragmented Curriculum

One of the most daunting problems facing teachers and schools, particularly at the high school level, is the absolutely overwhelming bloated and fragmented curriculum that they feel compelled "to cover." The standards movement has only made things worse in that regard. Bob Marzano (2003), in a thorough analysis of the curricula implied by state and national standards, has estimated that in fourteen subject areas, there are two hundred and fifty-five standards and three thousand, five hundred benchmarks requiring an estimated fifteen thousand, five hundred hours of instruction. The hours currently available for instruction in most systems, K–12, are nine thousand hours. Marzano concludes that in order to address the current bloated curriculum in America, schooling would have to be extended from K–12 to K–22 (p. 26). I don't know of many people who would look forward to spending their thirtieth birthday in high school. In Marzano's words, we are "awash in a sea of standards" (Keynote address at CASE Winter Leadership Conference, 2004).

The curriculum is not only bloated, but also fragmented. Tom Vander Ark, speaking at a high school summit in Colorado (Vander Ark, 2004), observed that in his experience, "comprehensive (as in comprehensive high school) is the opposite of coherence." His point is that in trying to do everything for everyone, the curriculum of the comprehensive high school lacks focus and coherence. A bloated and fragmented curriculum interferes with the high school's efforts to identify a core academic mission.

How do teachers cope with the bloated and fragmented curriculum facing them each year? They pick and choose among standards. What criteria do they base their decisions on? Who knows?

Larry Ainsworth (2003), advocating for an agreed-upon set of criteria for distinguishing essential standards from those that are simply nice to know, captures the reality of curriculum decision making in our schools: "In the absence of an agreed-upon set of criteria for prioritizing the standards and indicators, educators will, out of necessity, make up their own..., individual educators working in isolation from their colleagues" (p. 15). We can do better than that. We must do better than that if we are to avoid curriculum anarchy and work toward a core academic mission for our high schools. But how?

Creating a Core Academic Mission at Littleton High School

Littleton High School has used several different strategies to identify our core academic mission. During the Direction 2000 years, our core academic mission was clearly defined through a set of nineteen performance-based graduation requirements and the assessments that defined what good work looked like for each requirement (see Figures 16–18).

Figure 16

LITTLETON HIGH SCHOOL GRADUATION REQUIREMENTS	
Communication:	The LHS graduate speaks and writes articulately and effectively.
	The LHS graduate reads and listens actively.
	The LHS graduate uses another language, so as to appreciate the relationship between language and culture.
Community Involvement:	The LHS graduate has actively contributed to community or school service organizations.
Consumer Economics:	The LHS graduate understands the nature of economics as it applies to everyday living.
Critical Thinking:	The LHS graduate uses research and the problem solving process in various fields to qualify and quantify information, to make critical distinctions, and to arrive at a decision.
Ethics:	The LHS graduate understands the importance of ethical conduct.
Human Relations:	The LHS graduate interacts well and works cooperatively with others.
Literary Arts:	The LHS graduate reads and evaluates literature.

(cont'd.)

Figure 16 *(Continued)*

LITTLETON HIGH SCHOOL GRADUATION REQUIREMENTS

Mathematics:	The LHS graduate effectively applies mathematical principles and operations to solve a range of problems.
Personal Growth:	The LHS graduate evaluates his/her own goals and demonstrates self-discipline.
Personal Health:	The LHS graduate implements a plan for physical and mental health.
The Sciences:	The LHS graduate applies skills and scientific concepts to explain his/her world, to find solutions for its problems, and to suggest improvements in the quality of life.
Social and World Relationships:	The LHS graduate uses his/her knowledge of the past to explain the present and anticipate the future.
	The LHS graduate applies physical and cultural geography to his/her understanding of societies.
	The LHS graduate understands the structures, operations, and relationships of governments in the United States.
Technology:	The LHS graduate demonstrates a practical/knowledge of specific, current tools and technical systems used by society.
	The LHS graduate demonstrates an awareness of how his/her environment is affected by technology in everyday life.
Visual and Performing Arts:	The LHS graduate participates in and is aesthetically aware of the visual and performing arts.

Figure 17

COMMUNICATION I

Graduation Requirement:
The LHS graduate speaks and writes articulately and effectively.

Description:
The student writes and speaks using grammatically acceptable English; adjusts tone and style of writing and speaking for a variety of purposes and audiences; supports statements using well-founded facts, theory, and opinion; separates fact from opinion; logically reaches conclusions based on sufficient evidence; distils information and clearly and succinctly states key points; effectively organizes ideas in a variety of ways; and demonstrates creativity through style, organization, and development of content.

Figure 18

COMMUNICATION I: SPEAKING AND WRITING

Graduation Requirement:
The L.H.S. graduate speaks and writes articulately and effectively.

Specific Skills:
The student:
1) Adjusts style and tone to purpose and audience;
2) Supports statements using well-founded facts, theories, and opinions; logically reaches conclusions based on sufficient evidence;
3) Clearly states points effectively and organizes ideas;
4) Uses grammatically acceptable English.

Demonstration l: (1 of 4)

The student writes a letter to a public policy maker regarding the official's position on a current political issue, presenting the student's opinion and persuading the public policy maker to vote accordingly. This public policy maker is opposed to the student's position. Students will be provided documentation of public policy maker's position and background information. Student will be given a choice of several situations.

Testing Conditions:
♦ Under supervision of classroom teacher or approved proctor.
♦ Timed: Two (45 minutes each) periods. Materials left with proctor.
♦ No peer editing—self-editing only.
♦ Resources allowed: dictionary, thesaurus, computer, spellers, Writers INC.
♦ Background materials available at least one week before the two (45 minutes each) testing sessions:
    – Public record of policy maker's opinion.
    – Sample of letter format.
    – Samples of proficiency and excellence in content.

Standards:
Proficient:
♦ Letter is persuasive: writer clearly states an opinion, uses facts to support the opinion, and explains why the facts support the opinion.
♦ Acceptable letter format is used (i.e., Writers INC).
♦ Argument is "one-sided"—writer does not successfully use facts to refute the public policy maker's position.
♦ Basic organization of the letter is presentation of a problem and discussion of a solution.
♦ Wording and attitude are appropriately formal for writing a public policy maker.
♦ Few grammatical, punctuation, or spelling errors—these errors do not detract from the purpose or organization of the letter.

(cont'd.)

Figure 18 *(Continued)*

COMMUNICATION I: SPEAKING AND WRITING

Standards:

Proficient *(cont'd.)*:

♦ Vocabulary is sufficient, and the sentence structure is complex, but not varied.

Excellent:

♦ Letter is persuasive; writer clearly states an opinion, uses facts to support the opinion, and explains why the facts support the opinion.

♦ In addition, the writer also presents a "two-sided" argument explaining why the facts support the writer's opinion and refute that of the public policy maker.

♦ Writer often uses psychological motivator (Why you are off-the-wall if you don't support my position).

♦ Basic organization is presentation of a problem, discussion of a solution, and recommendation for an action.

♦ Wording and attitude are appropriately formal for writing a public policy maker.

♦ Letter is essentially free of grammatical, punctuation, and spelling errors.

♦ Vocabulary is interesting; sentence structure is varied.

Unacceptable:

The letter is deficient in one of the following ways:

♦ Not a persuasive letter (no opinion is stated; the opinion is stated but not supported by facts; or there is no explanation of how facts support the opinion).

♦ Basic organization lacks presentation of a problem followed by a solution.

♦ Inappropriate wording or attitude.

♦ More than a few errors in grammar, punctuation, or spelling.

♦ Weak vocabulary, poor sentence structure.

Essential Tasks as a Core Academic Mission

The Direction 2000 program ran into political opposition, which resulted in the demise of our performance-based graduation requirements in early 1994. Creativity sometimes arises out of adversity, and that is exactly what happened because the Littleton High School faculty were determined to find a way to identify the core curriculum for our school. The former demonstration tasks from the Direction 2000 program were revised and renamed "Essential Tasks." There were thirty-three of them in all, and they served to identify the most essential learnings at the course and department levels. Essential tasks, then, helped us narrow our curriculum because, instead of being awash in a sea of hundreds of standards and thousands of benchmarks, we could focus instruction on a core academic curriculum of thirty plus essential learnings. Sample essential tasks, in this case from the science department, are displayed in Figures 19 and 20.

Figure 19

SCIENTIFIC EXPERIMENTAL DESIGN RUBRIC
(EDR)

Feedback is provided for each component (a,b,c . . .) according to the following scheme: (2X) – value is double for this component

- ◆ 3   The requirement is fulfilled in entirety.
- ◆ 2   The requirement is partially fulfilled.
- ◆ 1   The requirement is minimally addressed.
- ◆ 0   The requirement is missing.

ABSTRACT: An abstract is a brief explanation of an experiment. Although it is the first section read, it is the last section written because it summarizes everything from the purpose of the experiment through the conclusion. After reading an abstract, the reader understands what was investigated, how the experiment was designed, what results were obtained, and what conclusion was drawn.

In your abstract,
   a. The experimental purpose is clear and focused.
   b. All independent and dependent variables and constant conditions are accurately identified.
   c. The method for data collection is summarized.
   d. Relevant results are summarized.
   e. The relationship between independent and dependent variables is clear and accurate and is supported by results.
   f. The conclusion relates to experimental purpose.
   g. The purpose, method, results, and conclusion are addressed in this order.

BACKGROUND INFORMATION: The background information provides sufficient content to the reader so that he or she can understand the purpose of the experiment, the design, and the interpretation of the results. The writer must research the background information and properly cite (APA documentation) all sources used. A brief summary of the purpose and the experimental design should be included at the end.

In your background information,
   a. (2X) The content is thoughtful and provides sufficient background information to understand experiment.
   b. The background information is clear, focused, and accurate.

(cont'd.)

Figure 19 *(Continued)*

SCIENTIFIC EXPERIMENTAL DESIGN RUBRIC
(EDR)

BACKGROUND INFORMATION (cont'd.):

In your background information,
   c. (2X) Relevant and accurate details are consistently used to support statements.
   d. Scientific ideas are confirmed with reliable sources.
   e. The purpose and method for data collection are clearly and accurately summarized.
   f. Sequencing progresses from general to specific.

PROBLEM STATEMENT: A problem statement describes what is being investigated and identifies variables and conditions being held constant.

In your problem statement,
   a. The purpose of experiment is accurately stated.
   b. All independent and dependent variables are accurately identified.
   c. All conditions held constant are accurately identified.
   d. The purpose, variables, and constants are addressed in this order.

HYPOTHESIS: A hypothesis uses scientific principles and/or prior knowledge to predict the outcome of how the independent variable will affect the dependent variable.

In your hypothesis,
   a. The expected outcome reflects purpose and is clearly stated.
   b. (2X) HOW the independent variable(s) is expected to affect each dependent variable is clearly explained.
   c. (2X) WHY this/these effect(s) is/are expected is clearly explained using scientific principles or prior knowledge.

DESIGN: The design of the experiment provides a plan to investigate the problem and test the predictions made in the hypothesis. It should include enough detail so that the experiment is reproducible. The experimental set-up and measurement techniques must be described.

In your design,
   a. The list of materials is complete and accurate.
   b. The relevant sizes, quantities and/or concentrations of equipment/materials are provided.
   c. The safety guidelines are appropriate for experiment and are clear and focused.
   d. (2X) The step-by-step procedure for data collection is clear, accurate, logically ordered, and includes enough detail to be reproducible.

(cont'd.)

Figure 19 *(Continued)*

SCIENTIFIC EXPERIMENTAL DESIGN RUBRIC
(EDR)

DESIGN (cont'd.):

In your design,
  e. (2X) The method for data collection includes detailed instructions for collection of all relevant qualitative and quantitative data.
  f. The procedure includes instructions for collection of multiple sets of data (i.e., repeated trials).
  g. The sequence of steps is in logical order.
  h. A detailed, labeled diagram is included.
  i. The design includes an appropriate control or justifies its absence.

RESULTS: The results of an experiment are a neat, well-organized presentation of observations and measurements.

In your results, the data
  a. Are presented clearly in well-organized tables.
  b. Are properly labeled.
  c. In table(s) reflect independent variable.
  d. Include all qualitative and quantitative observations.
  e. Are consistent with expected experimental results.
  f. Include appropriate metric units for all quantitative measurements.
  g. Show accurate uncertainty of measurements.

ANALYSIS: An analysis interprets the data collected. Relationships between variables are displayed on graphs, and/or data are processed using calculations to help the scientist use the data to evaluate the hypothesis. The evaluation of the hypothesis includes specific data, graphical relationships, or calculations. The effect of error on the results is analyzed, and improvements are suggested.

In your graph,
  a. The title includes all appropriate variables and reflects their relationship
  b. Variables are placed on appropriate axes
  c. Axes are labeled correctly
  d. Correct metric units are included
  e. Axes show natural progression of numbers
  f. Appropriate graphing style is used
  g. At least 2/3 of grid is used
  h. Data points are plotted accurately
  i. Graph is entirely computer generated

In your calculation section,
  a. (2X) Calculations performed are appropriate for evaluating hypothesis.

(cont'd.)

Figure 19 *(Continued)*

SCIENTIFIC EXPERIMENTAL DESIGN RUBRIC
(EDR)

ANALYSIS (cont'd.):

In your calculation section,
   b. Each category of calculation is correctly labeled.
   c. Each formula used is shown.
   d. All work is shown.
   e. Calculations are performed accurately.
   f. Each number includes an appropriate unit
   g. Appropriate number of significant figures is shown

In your interpretation of the results,
   a. The relationship between independent and dependent variable is summarized accurately referring to data, graphs, or calculations.
   b. The hypothesis is accurately summarized and evaluated.
   c. The evaluation of hypothesis is based on results.
   d. Reasonable sources of error are clearly stated and reflect results.
   e. The explanation of effect of error on results is accurate and specific.
   f. Realistic suggestions to improve data collection are provided.
   g. Validity of results is analyzed based on error.
   h. The variable relationship, evaluation of hypothesis, and discussion of error are addressed in this order.

CONCLUSION: The results of the experiment are related to an accepted scientific principle. The writer must research the scientific principle/concept and properly cite (APA documentation) all sources used. Suggestions to further study the topic are given.

In your conclusion,
   a. The experimental relationship between the independent and the dependent variable is evaluated using accepted scientific principles/concepts.
   b. The evaluation of the relationship is thoughtful and refers to results.
   c. Reliable sources are used to verify scientific principles/concepts.
   d. Suggestions for further study include modifications or extensions.
   e. The experimental relationship is addressed followed by suggestions for further study.

Figure 20

ARTICLE CRITIQUE
Anchor Document

Part I—Summary of Original Article and Research Plan

Student will

- Extract relevant information (identify main point and key statements).
- Rate reliability of source of original article.
- Develop research questions.
- Develop research plan.
- State and explain opinion on reliability of science being reported in original article.
- Write citation for original article.

Part II—Research

Student will

- Find three relevant research articles from scientific sources.
- Highlight or take notes on information that helps determine value of each research article (currency*, accuracy, authority of author, purpose/audience, point of view, fact vs. opinion).
- Describe (briefly) how each research article supports/rejects original article.

* Currency may vary depending on teacher requirements.

Part III—Evaluation of Original Article

Student will

- Evaluate main idea and key statements of original article using each research article.
- Evaluate reliability/good science/quality of original article using each research article.
- Explain final opinion on reliability of original article and compare final opinion to initial opinion.
- Describe effect of topic on self or community (explain personal meaning).

Power Standards

Essential Tasks worked okay, but over time we became more and more aware of the fact that a core curriculum defined at the course and department levels would not help us narrow our focus schoolwide. A chance exposure to Doug Reeves from the Center for Performance Assessment (CPA) presented a solution to our problem. In *101 Questions and Answers About Standards, Assessments, and Accountability*, Reeves (2001) offers his perspective on this "problem":

> Every school district in the nation has some form of local or state academic content standards. These standards describe what students are expected to know

and be able to do. The standards do not, however, give the classroom teacher and the school leader clarity about which standards are the most important for future success. Because of the limitations of time and the extraordinary variety in learning backgrounds of students, teachers and leaders need focus and clarity in order to prepare their students for academic success. (p. 167)

The solution that Reeves proposes is that schools identify a limited number of what he calls "power standards." Power standards are not intended to represent everything students will be taught in their high school careers, but rather those few things that form a network or connection among curricular objectives and that research has shown to be highly transferable across academic disciplines. Once mastered, according to Reeve's research, power standards enable students to be successful in their coursework and score well on standardized tests.

In reality, all standards are not created equal. As Ainsworth (2003) argues, certain standards are more important than others in terms of student success: "Power standards are *prioritized* standards that are derived from a systematic and balanced approach to distinguishing which standards are absolutely essential for student success from those that are 'nice to know'" (p. 3).

Reeves (2001) suggests three "screens" to identify power standards:

- ◆ "**Endurance**—will this provide students with knowledge and skills that will be of value beyond a single test date?
- ◆ **Leverage**—will this provide students with knowledge and skills that will be of value in multiple disciplines?
- ◆ **Readiness for the next level of learning**—will this provide students with essential knowledge and skills that are necessary for success in the next level of instruction?" (p. 169)

Ainsworth (2003) suggests a school, life, and state test set of criteria for identifying power standards: "What do your students need for success—in school (this year, next year, and so on), in life, and on your state tests?" (p. 16). He further operationalizes these criteria in the form of two "guiding" questions:

- ◆ "What essential understandings and skills do our students need?
- ◆ Which standards can be clustered or incorporated into others?" (p. 12)

Either set of criteria, Reeves' or Ainsworth's, and the accompanying guiding questions can be used effectively to help educators define a high school's core academic mission.

Ainsworth (2003) recounts Doug Reeves' illustration of how the process outlined above can be used to make standards more manageable by reorganizing one state's 87 middle school math standards into seven power standards:

- ◆ "All four number operations (add, subtract, multiply, divide) with and without calculators
- ◆ Two-dimensioned scale drawings

- Transform a word problem into an accurate picture representative of the problem
- Fraction, decimal, and percentage operations (add, subtract, multiply, divide)
- Measurement in standard and metric units
- Graphs, charts, tables (create them from row data, and draw inferences from them when presented)
- Properties of rectangles and triangles. (p. 12)

It sounds doable, doesn't it?

In the fall of 2001, the Littleton High School community launched an initiative for power standards designed to identify a limited number of school-wide standards that all teachers would focus on in all classes and that would help define our academic core mission. Today, the faculty have implemented Writing and Information Literacy power standards and are continuing the development of Critical Thinking/Reasoning and Citizenship/Work Habits power standards (see Figures 21–26). Of interest, futurist Gary Marx (2006) suggests "building media literacy skills," "helping students understand

Figure 21

LITTLETON HIGH SCHOOL WRITING STANDARD

Writing: Students write and speak effectively for a variety of purposes and audiences using proper conventions.

As students in grades 9–12 extend their knowledge, what they know and are able to do includes:

- Convey information in a written form appropriate to the audience;
- Select a clear and focused topic;
- Draft, revise, edit and proofread a legible final copy;
- Develop a main idea using relevant, accurate supporting details;
- Organize writing so that sequencing is logical and effective and transitions show how ideas are connected;
- Align voice, tone and style to further purpose and appeal to audience;
- Use specific and accurate words and phrases that are natural, effective, and appropriate;
- Incorporate and cite material from a wide range of sources (e.g., newspapers, magazines, interviews, technical publications, books) in their writing and speaking;
- Use conventional grammar, sentence structure, and mechanics (spelling, capitalization, punctuation).

Figure 22

ANCHOR DOCUMENT FOR WRITING POWER STANDARD						
	Ideas and Content	Organization	Voice	Word Choice	Sentence Fluency	Conventions
5	♦ Clear, focused topic ♦ Relevant and accurate supporting details	♦ Clear introduction, body, and satisfying conclusion ♦ Thoughtful transitions clearly show how ideas are connected ♦ Sequencing is logical and effective	♦ Tone furthers purpose and appeals to audience ♦ Appropriately individual and expressive	♦ Words are specific and accurate ♦ Language and phrasing is natural, effective, and appropriate	♦ Sentence construction produces natural flow and rhythm.	♦ Grammar and usage are correct and contribute to clarity and style
3	♦ Broad topic ♦ Support is generalized or insufficient	♦ Recognizable beginning, middle, and end ♦ Transitions often work well; sometimes connections between ideas are fuzzy ♦ Sequencing is functional	♦ Tone is appropriate for purpose and audience ♦ Not fully engaged or involved	♦ Words are adequate and support the meaning ♦ Language is general but functional	♦ Sentences are constructed correctly	♦ Grammar and usage mistakes do not impede meaning
1	♦ Unclear topic ♦ Lacking or irrelevant support	♦ No apparent organization ♦ Lack of transitions ♦ Sequencing is illogical	♦ Not concerned with audience or fails to match purpose ♦ Indifferent or inappropriate	♦ Improper word choice/ usage makes writing difficult to understand ♦ Language is vague or redundant	♦ Sentences are choppy, incomplete, or unnatural	♦ Grammar and usage mistakes distract the reader or impede meaning

Figure 23

POWER STANDARD—INFORMATION LITERACY
(Find It, Read It, Evaluate It, Use It)

Find It: Information Acquisition

- Formulates questions based on information needs (Colorado State Standard 1, Indicator 3-abbreviated CSS 1:3)
- Develops and uses successful strategies for locating a variety of information sources and information (CSS 1:4,5)
- Recognizes accuracy, currency, and comprehensiveness of available information (CSS 1:1)

Read It: Use of Literacy Skills and Strategies

- Prereads: previews, predicts, infers (CSS Literacy 5)
- Reads: identifies author's purpose, recognizes main idea; paraphrases, summarizes, organizes, synthesizes (CSS Literacy 5)
- Understands structure, organization, and use of variety of texts and genres (CSS Literacy 5)
- Determines meanings of words using contextual and structural clues (CSS Literacy 5)

Evaluate It: Critical Evaluation of Information

- Selects appropriate information (CSS 2:4)
- Determines accuracy, relevancy and comprehensiveness (CSS 2:1)
- Distinguishes among facts, point of view and opinion (CSS 2:2)
- Evaluates sources (CSS 4:2)

Use It: Applying Information to Make Meaning

- Organizes and integrates new information into one's knowledge (CSS 3:1,2)
- Applies information in critical thinking and problem solving (CSS 3:3)

---

how to build a case" (creative and critical-thinking skills), and "building an understanding of ethical behavior" as important components of a school curriculum that seeks to prepare students for the realities of the global knowledge/information age—three of Littleton High School's four power standards. The fourth standard, writing, is implied in several of his other recommendations (pp. 14–15).

These four power standards were developed by a committee of teachers, students, and parents and have taken the format, as you can see from Figures 21–26, of an initial document (see Figure 21, for example) that begins to define what is included in the power standard and then a second document (see Figure 22 or 24), which defines more specifically what good work in that

Figure 24

INFORMATION LITERACY POWER STANDARD INDICATORS

Information Literacy: the ability to identify, locate, evaluate, and use information in solving problems and composing discourse.

Task Definition

- Determines what is known and what is needed for problem solving
- Frames appropriate question(s) based on information needed to solve the problem or answer the question.

Information Seeking Strategies

- Determines possible range of sources (primary, secondary, print, electronic, internet, current vs. retrospective, popular vs. scholarly)
- Locates possible sources
- Expands or narrows search as needed
- Prioritizes sources according to relevancy

Evaluating Sources and Extracting Data

- Utilizes criteria for evaluating sources (currency, accuracy, authority, purpose/audience, point of view, facts vs. opinions)
- Selects information appropriate to the problem or question
- Applies principles of academic honesty when extracting data (note cards, bib-cards, source citations, works cited)

Synthesis/Product

- Uses retrieved information to answer question (thesis/hypothesis)
- Uses new information and prior knowledge to make inferences, connections, and conclusions
- Organizes information into a logical structure
- Demonstrates awareness of the value and limitations of the sources used in answering the question
- Applies principles of academic honesty when communicating data
- Communicates information in an appropriate format

---

area looks like. True to the intent of the term "power standards," expectation for the Writing power standard at Littleton High School is summarized by the expression, "every teacher, every class, every trait (of the rubric), every semester." All students receive instruction, feedback, and an opportunity to improve their writing in every class they take using expectations and language that are consistent across departments. Similar expectations will be in place in future years for each of the other three power standards. A system for monitoring the results of the Writing power standard is in

Figure 25

THINKING AND REASONING

The goal of incorporating thinking and reasoning skills into the LHS curriculum is to develop individuals who value knowledge, learning, and the creative process, and who can and will think for themselves. At Littleton High School, thinking and reasoning consist of the following skills:

- ◆ Evaluating Information
  - Assessing the reasonableness and quality of information (ideas)
  - Setting standards for making judgments
  - Confirming the accuracy of claims
- ◆ Identifying Similarities, Dissimilarities and Patterns
  - Comparing and contrasting
  - Analyzing relationships
  - Classifying
- ◆ Logic
  - Argumentation
  - Making inductions
  - Making deductions
- ◆ Investigation
  - Identifying what is known or what is commonly accepted about a concept
  - Identifying contradictions and points of confusion
  - Offering and defending solutions, or making and testing predictions related to the contradictions and points of confusion
- ◆ Problem Solving
  - Using appropriate trouble-shooting strategies
  - Isolating and reframing alternatives
  - Predicting, evaluating and defending a solution
- ◆ Decision Making
  - Investigating and defining alternatives
  - Predicting consequences of alternatives
  - Making personal and relevant decisions based on data and criteria

place that focuses on both standardized test scores and student and teacher self-assessments.

An example of the potential power of power standards is seen in an e-mail (Figure 27) sent to the chairperson of the power standards committee (a science teacher) from a member of the Littleton High School mathematics department following an Information Literacy power standard staff development

Figure 26

CITIZENSHIP/WORK HABITS

- Consistently meets assignment expectations
- Uses time efficiently and effectively
- Shows sufficient effort in class and on assignments
- Demonstrates a positive attitude
- Is willing to share, compromise, and work toward a goal alone or with others
- Is engaged, ready to respond—willing to respond
- Attends class regularly
- Accepts responsibility for own performance and actions
- Follows class and school procedures
- Demonstrates integrity in academic and interpersonal affairs
- Uses respectful speech toward others
- Respects cultural and social differences
- Shows a tolerance for other points of view
- Participates or engages in community service

---

session. Notice the focus on anchoring research with good questions. Notice the emphasis on writing (in math). Notice the integration of the two power standards—information literacy and writing.

The power standards project is expected to take ten years to implement fully, and if past experience is any guide, teachers will be anxious to revise their work based on what they have learned long before this time is over. This is an important message for leaders wishing to undertake a significant school improvement effort. Significant school improvement takes time. Improvements can be made in a year or two, but long-term transformation takes a long-term and focused commitment. Massive staff development is, of course, an important part of such a transformation, which was a topic discussed earlier in this book.

A Guaranteed and Viable Curriculum

Power standards and essential tasks are just two of many approaches a high school could use to identify a core academic mission. In *What Works in Schools: Translating Research into Action*, Bob Marzano (2003) identifies eleven factors validated by thirty-five years of research as having a positive effect on student achievement. The first factor, and the school-level factor with the greatest effect, is "A Guaranteed and Viable Curriculum." According to

Figure 27

E-MAIL ABOUT POWER STANDARDS

From: Weber Jacqueline
Sent: Monday, September 20, 2004, 2:34 PM
To: Mann Erin
cc: Westerberg Tim
Subject: Info Literacy In-service Dept. Mtg. Notes

Erin,

As requested, below is the summary of the meeting that the math department held Friday afternoon and the (very) useful documents we created. We spent a great deal of time revising our "Tombstone" project to make it less of a research project and more of an inquiry/discovery project. We also had a thorough conversation regarding how to better equip our students with the ability to ask "good questions." This line of inquiry also plays into our newly revised project.

In addition, we created rough outlines for three other smaller activities that develop researching, analysis, and creative questioning skills. We decided that we wanted to emphasize the Info. Lit. aspects of analysis, synthesis, and creating a product. We also reinforced with members the importance of integrating the writing literacy aspect into our activities and that not all products need to be giant research papers. We discussed numerous methods for the collection and use of statistics and how small exercises could help develop the Info. Lit. skills needed to attack the larger projects in our math classes and in the curriculum as a whole.

Finally, we developed a smaller stats project, which would present data and have the students formulate questions based on the data and how it could be further researched to answer more in-depth questions. This is one of our "lead up" tasks to help build the necessary skills.

Attached you will find the rough draft of our revised project. We will implement this project in the beginning weeks of October at as many levels as possible. Please contact me if you have any questions. Thank you!

Jackie Weber and Members of the Math Dept.

Marzano, a guaranteed and viable curriculum is one in which (1) clear guidance is given to teachers regarding what content to teach in specific courses and at specific grade levels, (2) individual teachers do not have the option to disregard or replace assigned content, and (3) the content assigned to a particular course or grade level can be adequately addressed in the time available (pp. 25–30). A high school that has successfully completed the very difficult but powerful process of identifying and operationalizing a guaranteed and viable curriculum, at the course level and perhaps at the department-, grade-, or school-level, has, in effect, established a core academic mission.

Is the content that is *guaranteed* to every student, regardless of which teacher the computer schedules the student with, clearly established in our high schools? Recall the quotation cited earlier by Jerald Craig (2003), regarding the state of curricular affairs in American schools:

> Decisions about what to teach in each grade are left up to schools, many of which pass the choice on to teachers. The result is an uneven hodgepodge of instructional aims and subject matter, with content and expectations varying sharply from classroom to classroom and from school to school. . . curriculum anarchy (p. 13)

A core academic mission does not exist in a school in which curriculum anarchy is allowed to go unchecked.

During a workshop in Denver in 2004, Rick and Becky DuFour suggested the following five-step process to establish a guaranteed and viable curriculum, or what I have been calling a core academic mission:

♦ "Clarify 8–10 essential outcomes per semester by course/content area;

♦ Develop at least 4 common assessments per year;

♦ Establish specific, measurable standards or goals;

♦ Analyze results; and

♦ Identify and implement improvement strategies."

Together, these five steps constitute a continuous improvement process, with the first two steps yielding a guaranteed and viable curriculum for a school. Figure 28 illustrates this process through the example of a course entitled

Figure 28

FORCED CHOICE MASTERY			
10-1: Inferential Reading			
ENG110FR English—Foley	T(00-01) - % Mean: 0.72-	(89%) 63 of 71 students have	
63	89% (15 of 25)	mastered this local standard. 80%	
8	11%		
ENG110FR English	(00-01) - % Mean: 0.73 -	(89%) 562 of 630 students have	
562	89% (15 of 25)	mastered this local standard. 80%	
68	11%		
10-2: Vocabulary Strategies			
ENG110FR English—Foley	T(00-01) - % Mean: 0.72	(61%) 43 of 71 students have	
43	61% (4 of 6)	mastered this local standard. 80%	
28	39%		
ENG110FR English	(00-01) - % Mean: 0.73	(73%) 458 of 630 students have	
458	73% (4 of 6)	mastered this local standard. 80%	
172	27%		

(cont'd.)

Figure 28 *(Continued)*

FORCED CHOICE MASTERY

10-3: Terms and Structured Literature

ENG110FR English—Foley	T(00-01) - % Mean: 0.72	(87%) 62 of 71 students have
62	87% (3 of 5)	mastered this local standard. 80%
9	13%	

ENG110FR English	(00-01) - % Mean: 0.73	(90%) 564 of 630 students have
564	90% (3 of 5)	mastered this local standard. 80%
66	10%	

10-4: Aims/Modes of Writing

ENG110FR English—Foley	T(00-01) - % Mean: 0.72	(80%) 57 of 71 students have
57	80% (5 of 9)	mastered this local standard. 80%
14	20%	

ENG110FR English	(00-01) - % Mean: 0.73	(78%) 491 of 630 students have
491	78% (5 of 9)	mastered this local standard. 80%
139	22%	

10-5: Correctness of Expression

ENG110FR English—Foley	T(00-01) - % Mean: 0.72	(79%) 56 of 71 Students have
56	79% (6 of 10)	mastered this local standard. 80%
15	21%	

ENG110FR English—	(00-01) - % Mean: 0.73	(73%) 458 of 630 students have
458	73% (6 of 10)	mastered this local standard. 80%
172	27%	

10-6: Identifying Phrases/Clauses

ENG110FR English—Foley	T (00-01) - % Mean: 0.72	(77%) 55 of 71 students have
55	77% (3 of 5)	mastered this local standard. 80%
16	23%	

ENG110FR English	(00-01) - % Mean 0.73	(83%) 520 of 630 students have
520	83% (3 of 5)	mastered this local standard. 80%
110	17%	

10:7: Identifying Sentences/Run-On/Fragments

ENG110FR English—Foley	T(00-01) - % Mean: 0.72	(86%) 61 of 71 students have
61	86% (3 of 5)	mastered this local standard. 80%
10	14%	

ENG110FR English	(00-01) - % Mean: 0.73	(86%) 543 of 630 students have
543	86% (3 of 5)	mastered this local standard. 80%
87	14%	

From DuFour, Rick, and Becky DuFour (2004); with permission.

"Freshman English" at Adlai Stevenson High School in Illinois. In this case, seven common outcomes have been assigned to all teachers teaching the course: Inferential Reading, Vocabulary Strategies, etc. It is also clear that all teachers share a common standard for mastery (80%) and that the data yielded by common assessments provides guidance in identifying areas in need of improvement.

School leaders at all levels across the country, and indeed in my former district, are taking on the important work of identifying a core (guaranteed) academic mission. Below are statements from elementary and middle school principals in the Littleton Public Schools in response to my question: "How are you establishing a guaranteed and viable curriculum in your school?" The responses suggest that both strategies and struggles are similar across levels.

Euclid Middle School

This is something we started working on two years ago with similar ideas of "a guaranteed and viable curriculum." The first area we attacked was math. It seemed to be the most straightforward and the easiest to bring to consensus. We started by asking our eighth grade teachers what they understood the high schools needed when our kids emerged from middle school. (It would have been more accurate to ask ninth grade teachers, but it usually slows up the process when we make it a districtwide issue.) Given these needs, we then asked each grade level what they needed from the previous grade. Then we were in a good position to influence the fifth grade exit test that was developed in the district the next spring.

We matched our grade level "essential outcomes" to CDE frameworks and LPS curriculum. It wasn't completely research-based but having a "guaranteed and viable curriculum" seemed more important than a perfect curriculum. We consider our "outcomes" to be in the draft mode.

Once we had these, we developed a pre/post test for every grade. I asked the teachers what they could guarantee to the next grade teachers. What will the kids know and be able to do? They agreed that our outcomes were "viable," and they could agree to take ownership for the students to learn them. They promised me and each other that the kids would learn the "EMS essential outcomes." We agreed that, as a team, we were responsible to take students from the end of fifth grade to the beginning of ninth grade. It would take all of us being faithful to the task to make all the kids successful.

We are beginning our third year of trying to accomplish this aim and are finding that the students are not learning the curriculum. We determined this by our own end of the year test, and it is supported by CSAP evidence. Now we are starting to question our instructional strategies in a very appropriate manner.

With this, the cycle of curriculum–assessment–instruction is coming full circle. Once we took ownership of it, we became determined to make the kids successful.

Centennial Academy of Fine Arts

Every year in the spring, we develop our week-by-week road maps at each grade level according to the LPS curriculum targets. As we discuss the delivery of these targets, we consider how well our plans worked during the year in light of benchmark assessments, ITBS, and anecdotal data. In the fall, we also gauge our effectiveness in light of our CSAP results, and we make adjustments to our road maps. While we use some programs, such as *Everyday Math*, we only follow them in the areas that support our curriculum.

Hopkins Elementary

Our school has been doing a lot of work in this area over the past nine months. We are using the work of the DuFours in identifying "Essential Learnings." These are the same as a guaranteed and viable curriculum. We are focusing all of our efforts on three questions:

- ♦ What do we want students to learn?
- ♦ How do we know if they learned it?
- ♦ What do we do if they don't learn it?

We have started identifying the guaranteed curriculum in the area of writing.

Options High School

All teachers have to think with the end in mind. Teachers have to submit a final exam at the beginning of the semester and the final they give at the end of the semester.

Teachers have to submit their course requirements. The requirements need to include course objectives for the class and how the students will demonstrate that they have achieved these objectives. The requirements also need to include how the students will be graded. The requirements need to be specific about how a student is to receive an A, B, C, D, and F. Are there required assignments to pass the class?

Teachers are required to turn in an outline on what will be covered in the class.

Finally our policy is to post good work so that other students can see what it looks like. Teachers keep examples from past years to show students good work on certain assignments they require.

Goddard Middle School

In Language Arts, our teachers have taken a look at the curriculum to determine what is really crucial. We map this out by grade level and ability level. (No small task, because we assess ability six ways for Language Arts: special education, ESL, low grade level, grade level, above grade level, and GT.)

All last year, middle level principals talked about the need for a "critical path" in the curriculum.

Creating a Culture of Collaborative Critical Reflection

If I were king and could change just one thing about the culture of the American high school, it would be to internalize in the day-to-day fabric of that culture the practice of teachers looking at student work together. In my opinion, everything else that needs to happen to change America's high schools, or at least nearly everything, would fall out from that one change. An *Education Week* article covering retiring superintendent Tom Payzant's success in turning around the Boston Public Schools has this to say about the levers of school improvement in the district: "The signature initiative is 'collaborative coaching and learning,' a process for teachers to hone their craft together by analyzing one another's work and the results of that work. It resembles how doctors in training learn to diagnose by working in groups to examine patients" (Archer, 2006, p. 31). But collaborative critical reflection has not been a characteristic of the American high school culture. What can we do to make it so?

A Focus on Student Achievement

Bob Marzano, Debra Pickering, and other members of the faculty of the Association for Supervision and Curriculum Development (ASCD) What Works in Schools are careful to emphasize that the focus of school improvement efforts must be squarely on measurable student achievement goals, and not on the interventions designed and implemented to reach those goals. Creating a culture of collaborative critical reflection in our high schools depends on our ability as leaders to keep the faculty focused on student achievement. A focus on student achievement should be at the center of our staff development efforts. That focus should direct what we talk about in our faculty meetings, influence our hiring and teacher-assignment decisions, and direct our budgeting decisions. A focus on student achievement should guide our selection of instructional materials and dictate the operation of our day and the structure of our school. A focus on student achievement, as illuminated through collaborative analysis of student work, must become a part of the culture of the American high school.

One of the reasons collaborative critical reflection does not happen in our high schools is that time for it is not built into the schedule. If we expect teachers to be enthusiastic about scheduling meetings with their colleagues for the purposes of analyzing and discussing student achievement at the end of a very exhausting school day, we expect what has never, and probably will never, happen. We have to find ways to build time for teacher talk into the schedule on a regular, ongoing basis. The leadership at Littleton High School has attempted to do this through course meetings, faculty meetings, professional development days, and paid summer work, an approach that receives greater attention later in this book.

The superior approach is that of building collaborative critical-reflection time into the school schedule on a weekly, bi-weekly, or monthly basis through either late starts or early dismissals. Englewood (Colorado) High

School, for example, schedules a half-day early dismissal each month for staff development purposes. Students at Wyandott (Kansas) High School are dismissed two hours early each Wednesday so that teachers can meet in small learning community study groups. Summit County School District (Colorado) dismisses students 30 minutes early once each week, which, combined with the hour already allocated for faculty meetings, produces 90 minutes of collaborative planning time weekly. An analysis of "breakthrough high schools"—high schools with at least a 50% minority population, 50% qualifying for free and reduced-priced meals, and at least 90% of the students graduating and accepted into college—found that several of those schools, including Crownpoint High School in New Mexico, Mabton Junior/Senior High School in Washington, and Poinciana High School in Florida, have weekly early-release time built into their schedules for targeted professional development. (Boone, Hartzman, and Mero, 2006, pp. 13, 32, and 44). Whatever the strategy, scheduling time for teachers to examine student work is essential to real school improvement.

Littleton High School's Experience

"What really distinguishes Bezos is his harrowing leaps of faith. His best decisions can't be backed up by studies or spreadsheets. He makes nervy gambles on ideas that are just too big and too audacious and too long-term to try out reliably in small-scale tests before charging in. . . . Bezos loves making decisions based on hard data, but when that's not possible, he believes in the power of being 'simpleminded,' relying on common sense about what would be in the best interests of his customers."

(Alan Deutschman, *Fast Company*, 2004, pp. 54 and 57)
writing about Amazon.com CEO, Jeff Bezos)

We hear much these days about data-driven decision making. I offer a slight twist on that thinking which I believe more accurately reflects how we ought to run our high schools—data-informed, but values driven. Of course we want to know what the data says about student achievement and about the quality of the learning environment at our school. But our values regarding what we believe to be true about the purpose of our work, about the kind of education we want our students to receive, about the learning theory that drives instruction in the school, about what the community wants for its children, about social progress and justice, and about the role of public education in a democratic society should drive the decisions we make. Inform me with data, but we will make decisions based on our values. We will be simpleminded, relying on common sense about what would be in the best interests of our students.

Tom Vander Ark of the Bill and Melinda Gates Foundation, speaking to a group of high school educators in Colorado, asked those in attendance, "Do your students understand what good work looks like in your school? Do teachers and students own 'what good' looks like?" (Keynote speech, 2004). At Littleton High School teachers look at many different types of data, including student achievement scores from standardized achievement and placement tests. But what they are most interested in is student work tied to the school's core academic mission as defined in essential tasks and building-wide power standards. In other words, the faculty at Littleton High School want to clearly define "what good work looks like" and then base decisions on it's values as informed by actual student work.

As has already been mentioned, time for collaborative critical reflection focused on actual student work, student work related directly to our core academic mission, is provided at Littleton High School through course-level and department meetings, faculty meetings, professional development days, and paid summer work.

Course- and department-level meetings provide an opportunity for teachers to work collaboratively to determine exactly what it is that they want our students to know and be able to do in particular courses and through the collection of courses taken in a particular department (essential learnings/tasks). They also provide time for teachers to determine what good work looks like in a course or department and to examine student work to determine to what extent we are reaching our academic goals. The notion that major outcomes of courses and the type and quality of work expected from students relative to those outcomes can, or even should, vary from teacher to teacher under the banner of academic freedom is just wrong. That is a condition that Craig Jerald (2003) calls curriculum anarchy:

> Decisions about what to teach in each grade are left up to schools, many of which pass the choice on to teachers. The result is an uneven hodgepodge of instructional aims and subject matter, with content and expectations varying sharply from classroom to classroom and from school to school . . . curriculum anarchy. (p. 13)

When I came to Littleton High School, teachers in our mathematics department had a rule stipulating that students could not move on to the next course in a sequence if they had not received at least a "C" in the prerequisite. I do not have a problem with that rule. It makes some sense to me that a student is not going to do well in Algebra II if he or she has not mastered important Algebra I content and skills. But when I asked teachers just exactly what it was that a student must know and be able to do in each of these courses (geometry, for example) in order to get a "C" or above and move on, I was met with confused looks and responses such as, "Well, they just have to get at least a seventy percent in my class." That was completely unacceptable to me. I insisted that teachers in the math department get together and decide what exactly it is that a student needs to know and be able to do in each case to move on and what evidence we will accept as proof of mastery of that knowledge and of those skills.

Another example comes from the social studies department, where, until recently, Littleton High School had a senior-level semester course that was so important to our students, so important to our school, so important to our democratic society, I guess, that it was a graduation requirement for students. When I asked the teachers of that course, "What exactly is it about Political and Economic World Issues that is important for every student to master, and what does good student work look like in each of those areas?" I was, once again, met with less than satisfying responses—curriculum anarchy. In that case, the teachers chose to restructure our social studies curriculum and discontinue the course rather than agree on major outcomes and assessments.

From time to time, a student or parent raises a question about the extent to which we have our act together regarding standards for student performance. That most recently came in the form of two students in the same course, but with different teachers, who received exactly the same semester percentages, but received different semester course grades. In that particular case, the parents wanted me to insist upon a common grading scale across the building. I refused to do that because I do not believe that a grading scale, in and of itself, solves the problem. What does an eighty-five percent tell you if teachers have not agreed on major outcomes and on what good work looks like? In my opinion, very little. In cases such as this, I insisted that the teachers get together to hammer out key outcomes and evidence of student mastery. I followed up a few weeks later with those teachers to ensure that the work had been completed or was at least underway. It did not always make me popular, but having the same body of evidence (student work) get different grades from different teachers of the same course is simply indefensible. Course-level and department meetings need to be used, in part, to reach those kinds of agreements and understandings.

Often, collaboration of this nature is too big in scope to accomplish during course and department meetings. If funds can be found, paid summer work for groups of teachers can offer a solution to this problem. At Littleton High School teachers are paid $100 per day for collaborative curriculum and assessment work, far below their contracted per diem salary. It is a compromise born of fiscal necessity that provides teachers with some compensation for work that needs to be done anyway and for administrators with the rationale for expecting a "product."

I always adjusted the building budget in whatever ways were necessary to provide funding for teachers to want to engage in this type of collaboration during the summer. Stalling progress in identifying a guaranteed curriculum for lack of a few hundred, or even a few thousand, dollars is penny wise and pound foolish.

Professional development time, including faculty meetings, provides opportunities for teachers to engage in collaborative critical reflection focused on student work. Rick DuFour (2004) asks us to consider our answers to four questions about professional development in our schools:

♦ "Does the professional development increase the staff's collective capacity to achieve the school's vision and goals?

♦ Does the school's approach to professional development challenge staff members to act in new ways?

♦ Does the school's approach to professional development focus on results rather than activities?

♦ Does the school's approach to professional development demonstrate a sustained commitment to achieving important goals?" (pp. 63–64)

Stephanie Hirsch (2004) of the National Professional Development Council, speaking to a group of high school educators in Colorado, argued that a results-driven ("results-informed" at Littleton High School) professional development program starts with the answers to these three questions:

♦ "What do students need to know and be able to do?

♦ What do educators need to know and be able to do to ensure student success?

♦ What professional development will ensure educators acquire the necessary knowledge and skills?"

Littleton High School's professional development planning and implementation is designed with these sets of questions in mind.

At Littleton High School, every minute of every faculty meeting (except for one each year in which the superintendent addresses the staff) and every minute of every professional development day is tied directly to the advancement of one or more of our four building goals. The four building goals, by the way, are power standards, literacy, at-risk students, and student advisement. Professional development is planned, starting a year in advance, by a group consisting of the administrative team and the teachers who chair each of our four building goals committees. An examination of Figure 29, a schedule for the last part of the 2003–04 professional development year, reveals a focus on literacy, writing, at-risk students, and student advisement (transition). It also reveals considerable time devoted to collective analysis of student work (e.g., program evaluation, data collection/evaluation, compilation of department [writing] exemplars, and interdepartmental inter-rater reliability). As Stephanie Hirsch (2004) so clearly stated in her speech at the CASE High School Summit, "Training without follow up is malpractice."

Littleton High School attempts to develop a professional development program that is responsive to both DuFour's and Hirsch's questions and that

Figure 29

SCHEDULE FOR PROFESSIONAL DEVELOPMENT			
March 31 **Faculty Meeting**	**April 28** **Faculty Meeting**	**May 25** **(6 hours)**	**May 26** **(3 hours)**

♦ Evolution of Writing P.S. evaluation plan
♦ Writing P.S.
  • Student self-assessment
  • Teacher evaluation
♦ Expectations for program evaluation
	♦ Colorado Basic Literacy Act and Individual Literacy Plans at LHS	**WRITING P.S.**
		♦ Data collection/ evaluation (1 hr)
		♦ Compilation of dept. exemplars (1 hr)
		♦ Interdeptmental inter-rater reliability (1 hr)
		♦ Dept. goals for literacy 04–05 (1.5 hr)
		♦ Timeline for devel-opment and imple-mentation of power standards (.5 hr)
		
		LUNCH—BBQ in the courtyard!
		
		TRANSITION PROGRAM
		♦ Format and expectations (1 hr)
			AT-RISK
			♦ 2003–04 F. Academy data shared (.5 hr)
			♦ Presentation of Transition Plan (.5 hr)
			♦ Discuss/present 04–05 Plan of Attack (.5 hr)
			♦ Teachers meet in professional learning groups to discuss/ debrief March 5 in-service. (1 hr)
			
			SEND OFF
			♦ T.W. paints a picture of what we have done in 03–04 and where we are going in 04–05 (.5 hr)

FALL 2004 ACTIVITIES
1. Disposition of Speaking Standard (1 hr)
2. Information Literacy P.S.
    a. Departmental discussions around assignments and activities.
    b. Approval of anchor document
3. At Risk
    a. Review Plan of Attack for 2004–05
    b. Review staff input from May

provides for adequate follow up to training. Our closing session in May 2004, for example, featured some very honest sharing among small interdepartmental groups of teachers regarding both successes and frustrations with our Writing power standard. Those discussions were structured by guiding questions prepared for the groups in advance and were focused on both exemplars of student writing and the results of teacher and student self-assessments. Professional development work earlier in the year engaged teachers in the same kind of examination of student writing, only at the departmental instead of interdepartmental level.

The professional development program at Littleton High School increases the faculty's capacity to achieve the school's vision and goals, challenges faculty members to act in new ways, focuses on results rather than activities, and is the result of sustained commitment to specific school goals. It addresses what students and teachers need to know. Littleton High School has not yet "arrived" with regard to internalizing the notion of regular collaborative critical reflection based on student work into the school culture. But the faculty has come a long way, largely because of the time we provide for this work and the structure and focus of course and department meetings, faculty meetings, professional development sessions, and paid summer work.

Standards-Based Grading

Closely related to the important issue of teachers' collaboratively establishing what constitutes mastery of course outcomes or power standards are issues related to grading and grade reporting. Guskey (1994, 1996), Marzano (2000), and Reeves (2004) are among the writers and researchers who have raised serious questions about the philosophical assumptions that underlie how grades are determined, as well as about the mathematical methods used to calculate them. Guskey, for example, reveals the disparity with regard to the purposes of grades typically found in any group of teachers, even teachers from the same school. In a workshop activity entitled, "What Grade Do Students Deserve?" Guskey asks participants to determine which of three grading methods (average score, median score, or deleting the lowest score) is fairest for seven students with very different circumstances. Consensus among participants is seldom achieved. Both Guskey and Reeves offer alternatives to the devastating practice of assigning zeros for work not turned in.

Bob Marzano (2000) identifies three problem areas with the current grading system that he says constitute a mandate to change:

- "Teachers consider many factors other than academic achievement when they assign grades;
- Teachers weight assessments differently; and
- Teachers misinterpret single scores on classroom assignments." (p. 3)

Because of these and other problems, Marzano writes, "Grades are so imprecise that they are almost meaningless" (p. 1).

Discussions of grades and reporting at Littleton High School center on four practices that I consider to be very questionable:

- Assigning Zeros: The practice of assigning zeros for incomplete work or for work not turned has already been questioned here. First, is it usually true that a student who has been in class at least part of the time or who has started but not completed a project knows nothing? A zero in the grade book would suggest that. Second, consider the mathematical effect of averaging a zero with, let's say, a 100% on an assignment of equal importance. The student still has an F (50%). Reeves and Guskey suggest, among other things, using a four-point grading scheme (4, 3, 2, 1) instead of a 100-point scale, assigning a 50% to work not turned in, or assigning incompletes as alternative strategies.

♦ Cumulative Grades: Should a student who struggled at the beginning of the course and received Ds on tests but who gets it together by the end of the semester and is doing A work receive a C, the average of those grades? Depending on the nature of the course, my answer might very well be "no." In a course with a dependent sequence of knowledge and skills, such as is the case with most mathematics classes for example, I would give that student an A since and A most accurately describes her knowledge of course content. The fact that she did not understand the material at the beginning of the course is irrelevant.

♦ Mixing Academic and Nonacademic Factors: Demonstrated mastery of key course outcomes? It's in there. Completion of homework? It's in there. Penalties for being tardy? They're in there. Class participation? It's in there. The "Prego approach" to grading significantly weakens the communicative power of the symbol. What does a C in chemistry mean? He knows his chemistry but refused to do the homework, or he thinks the periodic table is something you eat on, but is a nice kid and tries hard?

♦ Extra Credit: What is the logic behind substituting something "extra" in the curriculum for that which has been determined to be essential? I have seen the notion of standards-based grading being egregiously violated by granting extra credit in a science class, for example, for supporting the home team through attendance at a state athletic event. Attending a play could be awarded credit in an English or drama class if it was tied directly to essential course outcomes. But then it wouldn't be "extra" would it? Extra (additional) opportunities to demonstrate mastery of the guaranteed curriculum—yes. Extra credit for work or accomplishments outside the curriculum—curriculum anarchy.

The faculty at Littleton High School is talking about reporting, on report cards and on transcripts, two grades—one representing demonstrated mastery of key content and skills (the guaranteed curriculum) and one reflecting behaviors consistent with the components of the Citizenship/Work Habits power standards. Both pieces of information are important and should be reported, but they do not belong together.

Standards-based grading, as piloted by teachers throughout the Littleton Public Schools under the leadership of former professional development director, Debra Pickering, has great potential for addressing many of the issues related to grading and reporting. Figure 30 is an example from Pickering of how a report card might look in a standards-based grading system. *Transforming*

Figure 30

STANDARDS-BASED GRADING												
Learning Goals	Writing—Org.				Writing—Mech.				Reading Comprehension			Homework	
Assignments and Assessments	Para-Hobby 10/1	Text. P. 33 10/7	Compare 10/9	Final Compare	Para-Hobby 10/1	Compare 10/9	Final Compare	Grammar Wksht. 10/22	Pre Test 10/16	Strat. Wksht. 10/23	Assess. 10/28	Wk. 10/1	Wk. 10/8
Students	Social Studies Para. 10/22											Wk. 10/15	Wk. 10/23
Josh	3.7	3.7	4.0	3.3	3.7	2.3	2.7	3.0	2.0	2.0	2.0	2,3	2
	3.7			3.7									
Jamal	1.7	2.0	3.3	3.3	2.3	2.3	3.7	3.7	1.7	2.3	2.3		
	3.3			3.3									
Janie	3.7	4.0	3.3	1.3	4.0	1.3	2.0	2.0	2.0	2.3	2.0	1,1	1
	3.7			3.7									

Classroom Grading (Marzano 2000) is an excellent resource for an extensive review of alternatives to current grading practices.

Most high schools have, by now, made at least some attempt to align curricula with state standards, if for no other reason than because of NCLB requirements. Many schools and districts now send their teachers into battle with impressive and well-thought-out standards-based curriculum documents as armor in the fight against ignorance. The problem is that the armor is so heavy and bulky that it actually imprisons, rather than frees, the would-be conqueror, severely limiting his or her ability to adapt to field conditions in an effort to "leave no child behind."

Creating a standards-based curriculum is only the first step in moving to standards-based education. Taking the standards movement from the board room to the high school classroom is a mission in search of leadership. Leadership is needed to help teachers turn the present bloated and fragmented standards-based impossible dream into a guaranteed and viable curriculum. Leadership is needed to shift the focus of our thinking from what is taught to what is learned—from a focus on coverage to a focus on standards. Leadership, exercized by principals as well as teachers, is needed to create the high schools of our choice—standards-based schools in pursuit of a shared core academic mission.

Epilogue

Creating the Future

Yogi Berra is reported to have said, "Prediction is very difficult, especially about the future." Difficult as it may be, I'm going to make a prediction. High schools in America will emerge from present challenges as stronger and more viable institutions than ever before in their history. Why am I so confident?

First, Americans will not let high schools slip into extinction. The institution of the American high school is too much a part of our collective psyche. Americans grow up in high schools. Mention "school" to adults, and they think, most quite fondly, of their high school years. High schools are where young people learn what it means to be an American. Despite the growth of private education and home schooling, ninety percent of all adults are still educated in public high schools. Tremendous support for high schools, and particularly for public high schools, exists in this country. They're too important for us to let them fail.

My confidence in the future of the American high school stems, too, from the fact that we know enough to close the gap in our high schools between common sense and common practice. Education research of the last thirty-five years gives us the raw materials. Leadership is needed to fashion these raw materials into the high schools of our choice.

Where will that leadership come from? Clearly, policy makers and stakeholders at all levels, from parents and teachers to elected state and national leaders, will need to respond to the leadership call to action. But the keys to the high schools of the future are, as they should be, in the hands of today's and tomorrow's high school principals. America's high schools need leaders with the skills, the courage, and the moral commitment and resolve to open the doors to the future. America's high schools need principals who are willing to take charge of their own professional destinies. It is those principals who will determine the destiny of the American high school.

This book is about possibilities, the possibilities that are born out of the union of research, commitment to moral purpose, and leadership. We know a great deal about the purposes, cultures, structures, and strategies of schools in which teachers and students want to work and learn, and about the leadership necessary to create those schools. The time is right to turn possibilities into realities and to create the high schools of our choice for all of America's high school youth. The time is right, in the words of Sitting Bull, to "put our minds together and see what kind of life we can make for our children."

About Littleton High School

Littleton High School is best described as a suburban school with urban characteristics. Although Littleton would be described by most who know it as an "upscale," middle- and upper-class community, the "Broadway corridor" on which Littleton High School is located, just south of the Denver city limits, contains features—low-income housing, an ethnically and socioeconomically diverse population, neighborhood gangs—that give the student body a more urban look and feel than is true of the community overall. Littleton High School continues to enjoy a reputation as one of the top performing schools in the state, a reputation the school has earned in the nearly fifty years it has been at its present location and the more than 100 years that the school has existed as a separate entity. For at least the past twenty years, Littleton High School has been a leader in implementing standards-based education (rigor), programs and practices that personalize education (relationships), and a constructivist learning theory (relevance).

The information that follows is intended to give the reader some insight into both the characteristics and the academic achievement of Littleton High School's student body.

- Littleton High School is a suburban school with urban characteristics.
- Littleton High School serves approximately 1600 students in grades 9–12.
- Thirty-four percent of our student body consists of out-of-district students.
- Nineteen percent are minority students.
- Fourteen percent qualify for free or reduced lunch.
- Thirteen percent of LHS students receive special education services.
- Ten percent are second language learners.
- Between eighty-five and ninety percent of our seniors plan to attend college after graduation.
- The graduation rate is between ninety-five and ninety-six percent each year.
- Littleton High School has one of the highest IB diploma rates in the world—ninety-six percent.

- Ninety-six percent of all International Baccalaureate (IB) tests taken by Littleton High School students last spring received a score of "4" or above (passing).

- Fifty percent of all Advanced Placement (AP) tests taken last spring received a score of "3" or above (passing).

- One hundred ninety-six students took the SAT in 2005. The average verbal score was 565, and the average math score was 571, equaling a composite score of 1136. Corresponding composite scores for Colorado and for the nation were 1104 and 1026, respectively.

- Three hundred four students took the ACT in 2005 and received a composite score of 21.6. That compares to a state composite of 19.7 and a national composite of 20.9.

- The total Per Pupil Expenditure in 2004 was about $7,000.

References

"The Adviser System." Northfield, IL: New Trier Communications, 2003. Available at www.newtrier.k12.il.us/services/advisery

Ainsworth, Larry. *Power Standards: Identifying Standards That Matter Most.* Englewood, CO: Advanced Learning Centers, Inc., 2003.

American Institutes for Research and SRI International. *The Gates Foundation National School District and Network Grants Program, Year 2 Evaluation Report.* Washington, D.C., and Menlo Park, CA: American Institutes for Research and SRI International, 2004.

American Institutes for Research and SRI International. *The Gates Foundation National School District and Network Grants Program, Year 3 Evaluation Report.* Washington, D.C., and Menlo Park, CA: American Institutes for Research and SRI International, 2005.

American Youth Policy Forum, "High Schools of the Millennium." August 2000.

Archer, Jeff. "Time on His Side." *Education Week* 25, no. 39 (June 2006): 31.

Balfanz, Robert, and Nettie Legters. "Closing 'Dropout Factories': The Graduation-Rate Crisis We Know, and What Can Be Done About It." *Education Week* 25, no. 42 (July 2006): 42–43.

Berra, Yogi. Available at http://www.amusingfacts.com/cgi-bin/surf/surf_pass.cgi?template=sq.html&cfile=y.html.

Berry, Bertice. Keynote address, *Finding Your Purpose: At Home, At Work and in the Community*, The Principals' Partnership 2004 Summer Leadership Institute, July 12, 2004.

Boone, Elizabeth, Marlene Hartzman, and Dianne Mero. "Believing in Student Achievement." *Principal Leadership*, Special Edition (July 2006): 21–25.

Boone, Elizabeth, Marlene Hartzman, and Dianne Mero. "Breakthrough High Schools." *Principal Leadership*, Special Edition (June 2006): 12, 32, and 44.

Borsuk, Alan J. "Kati Haycock 'Takes Five.'" *Milwaukee Journal Sentinel* (6 July 2006): 2.

Boston Plan for Excellence. "Relationships Matter." *Focus on Children* 1 (SY2004–2005): 1–3.

Breaking Ranks II: Strategies for Leading High School Reform. Reston, VA: NASSP, 2004.

Bridgeland, John M., John J. Dilulio, and Karen Burke Morison. *The Silent Epidemic: Perspectives of High School Dropouts.* Washington, D.C.: Civic Enterprises, 2006.

Champeau, Ryan. "Doing Advisories." *Principal Leadership* 6, no. 7 (March 2006): 22–26.

Collaborative Communications Group, Inc. *A Theory of Action for High School Reform: A Conversation with Alan Bersin.* New York: Schools for a New Society, Carnegie Corporation of New York, 2006.

Colorado Commission for High School Improvement. "Principles for High School Reform." *Colorado Children's Campaign*. Denver, Colorado: Colorado Commission for High School Improvement, 2005.

Covey, Stephen. *The Seven Habits of Highly Effective People: Powerful Lessons in Personal Change*. New York: Simon & Schuster, 1989.

Craig, Jerald. "Beyond the Rock and the Hard Place." *Educational Leadership* 61, no. 3 (November 2003): 12–16.

David, Jane L., and Larry Cuban. *Cutting through the Hype: A Taxpayer's Guide to School Reforms*. Ms. Morris, IL: Education Week Press, 2006.

Deal, Terrence, and Kent D. Peterson. *Shaping School Culture: The Heart of Leadership*. San Francisco: Jossey-Bass, 1999.

DePree, Max. *Leading Without Power: Finding Hope in Serving Community*. San Francisco: Jossey-Bass, 1997.

Deutschman, Alan. "Inside the Mind of Jeff Bezos." *Fast Company* 85 (August 2004): 52–58.

DiMartino, Joseph P. "Personalized Learning." *NewsLeader*, January 2006, pp. 5 and 11.

Downy, C., B. Steffy, F. English, L. Frase, and W. Poston, W. *The Three-Minute Classroom Walk-Through*. Thousand Oaks, CA: Corwin Press, 2004.

DuFour, Rick, and Becky Burnette. "Pull Out Negativity By Its Roots." *Journal of Staff Development* 23, no. 3 (Summer 2002): 27–30.

DuFour, Rick. "The Best Staff Development is in the Workplace, Not in a Workshop." *National Staff Development Council* 25, no. 2 (Spring 2004): 63–64.

DuFour, Rick, and DuFour, Becky. "Professional Learning Communities." Workshop presented in Denver, CO, 29 September 2004.

Elmore, Richard F. "A Plea for Strong Practice." *Educational Leadership* 61, no. 3 (November 2003): 6–10.

Executive Summary: Evaluation of the Bill & Melinda Gates Foundation's High School Grants, 2001–2004. The National Evaluation of High School Transformation. Available at http://www.air.org, 2005.

Ferguson, Ronald F. "Paying for Public Education: New Evidence of How and Why Money Matters." *Harvard Journal on Legislation* 28 (Summer 1991): 465–498.

"Francis W. Parker Charter Essential School Advisory Program, 2004–2005." Paper presented at the High School Showcase in Warwick, RI, 2–3 February 2005.

Freidman, Thomas L. *The World is Flat: A Brief History of the Twenty-First Century*. New York: Farrar, Straus and Giroux, 2005.

"From the Top: Superintendents on Instructional Leadership." Report of a National Survey among Superintendents conducted for *Education Week* by Belden, Russonello, and Stewart (July 2005). Available at http://www.edweek.org/media/report-final.pdf

Fullan, Michael. *Leading in a Culture of Change*. San Francisco: Jossey-Bass, 2001.

Gehring, John. "Report Examines Motivation Among Students." *Education Week* 23, no. 15 (December 2003): 5.

Gradet, Howard. "Maximizing Professional Development." *Principal Leadership*, Special Edition (June 2006): 16–20.

Guskey, T.R., ed. *Communicating Student Learning: 1996 Yearbook of the Association for Supervision and Development*. Alexandria, VA: Association for Supervision and Development, 1996.

Guskey, T.R. "Making the Grade: What Benefits Students?" *Educational Leadership* 52, no. 2 (1994): 14–20.

Heifetz, Ronald A., and Marty Lensky. *Leadership on the Line: Staying Alive through the Dangers of Leading*. Boston: Harvard Business School Press, 2002.

Heifetz, Ronald A. and Marty Lensky. "When Leadership Spells Danger." *Educational Leadership* 61, no. 7 (April 2004): 33–37.

Hirsch, Stephanie. Keynote address at CASE High School Summit, Copper Mountain, Colorado, 11 June 2004.

Honawar, Vaishali. "A Union Chief's Defeat Stirs Debate on Leadership." *Education Week* 25, no. 40 (14 June 2006): 7.

Hupfeld, Kelly. "Remediation in Higher Education: What It Means for Colorado School Leaders." *CASE Leadership Series*. Colorado Association of School Executives, Summer 2006.

Institute for Educational Leadership. *Leadership for Student Learning: Redefining the Teacher as Leader*. Washington, D.C.: Institute for Educational Leadership, 2001.

Jones, Ken. "A Balanced School Accountability Model: An Alternative to High-Stakes Testing." *Phi Delta Kappan* 85, no. 8 (April 2004): 584–590.

Keller, B. "Principal Matters." *Education Week* 18, no. 11 (11 November 1998): 25–27.

Keller, Bess. "Miami's Board-Certified Teachers Advance Agenda." *Education Week* 25, no. 1 (31 August 2005): 3, 19.

Keller, Bess. "NBPTS Upgrades Profession, Most Agree, Despite Test-Score Letdown." *Education Week* 25, no. 40 (14 June 2006): 1 and 14.

Keller, Bess. "Teachers Recruited to Find Solutions to Vexing Policy Issues." *Education Week* 25, no. 42 (12 July 2006): 7.

Kirst, Michael W. *Overcoming the High School Senior Slump: New Educational Policies*. Washington, D.C., and San Jose, CA: The Institute for Educational Leadership and The National Center for Public Policy and Higher Education, 2001.

Langer, Judith A. *Effective Literacy Instruction: Building Successful Reading and Writing Programs*. Urbana, IL: National Council Teachers of English, 2002.

Lawrence-Lightfoot, Sara. *Respect: An Exploration*. Reading, MA: Perseus Books, 1999.

Lawrence-Lightfoot, Sara. Interview with David Gergen. *Online News Hour* 30 (June 1999). Available at http://www.pbs.org/newshour/gergen/june99/respect_6-30

Leithwood, K., and C. Riehl. "What we know about successful school leadership" (a report by Division A of the American Educational Research Association). Philadelphia: Temple University, Laboratory for Student Success, 2003.

LINK Program. Available at www.boomerangproject.com.

The Lost Opportunity of the Senior Year: Finding a Better Way. National Commission on the High School Senior Year. ERIC# ED453604. Education Resources Information Center, 2001. Available at http://ERICWebPortal/Home.portal?_nfpb=true&_pageLabel=RecordDetails...

Marx, Gary. *Sixteen Trends: Their Profound Impact on our Future*. Alexandria, VA: Educational Research Service, 2006.

Marzano, Robert J. Keynote address at CASE Winter Leadership Conference, Denver, Colorado, January 2004.

Marzano, Robert J. *What Works in Schools: Translating Research Into Action*. Alexandria, VA: ASCD, 2003.

Marzano, Robert J. *Transforming Classroom Grading*. Alexandria, VA: ASCD, 2000.

Marzano, R., T. Waters, and B. McNulty. *School Leadership that Works: From Research to Results*. Alexandria, VA, and Aurora, CO: ASCD and McREL, 2005.

Matthews, Jay. "2003 List: The Top High Schools." *Newsweek*. Available at http://www.msnbc.msn.com/id/6362098/site/newsweek/print/1/displaymode/1098/

McCarthy, Martha, and George D. Kuh. "Are Students Ready for College? What Student Engagement Data Say." *Phi Delta Kappan* 87, no. 9 (May 2006): 664–669.

Mitchell, Nancy. "School Reform Ideas Abound." *Rocky Mountain News* (13 November 2004): 21A.

National Association of Secondary School Principals. *Breaking Ranks II: Strategies for Leading High School Reform*. Reston, VA: NASSP, 2004.

National Research Council. "Engaging Schools: Fostering High School Students' Motivation to Learn." Report in *Education Week* (10 December 2003).

Noguera, Pedro A. "Transforming High Schools." *Educational Leadership* 61, no. 8 (May 2004): 26–31.

Norton, John. "Our First Conversation: What Does It Mean to Be a Teacher Leader?" *Teacher Leaders Network* (March 24–26, 2003). Available at http://www.teacherleaders.org/images/chat1excpt.pdf

Olson, Lynn. "Opening Doors." *Education Week* 25, no. 41S (22 June 2006): 24.

Overholt, Alison. "Listening to Starbucks." *Fast Company* (July 2004): 50–56.

Peterson, Kent D. "Positive or Negative." *Journal of Staff Development* 23, no. 3 (Summer 2002): 10–15.

Pope, Neta, Arlene Metha, and L. Dean Webb. *The Personal Adult Advocate Program*. Reston, VA: NASSP, 1997.

Putnam, Robert. *Remarks by the President and Participants in First Session of Economic Summit*. Washington, D.C.: White House Publications, 5 April 2000.

Quint, Janet. *Meeting Five Critical Challenges of High School Reform: Lessons from Research on Three Reform Models*. New York: MDRC, 2006.

Raising our Sights: No High School Senior Left Behind. Final Report of the National Commission on the High School Senior Year. Princeton, NJ: The Woodrow Wilson National Fellowship Foundation, 2001.

Reeves, D. *101 Questions and Answers About Standards, Assessments, and Accountability*. Denver, CO: Advanced Learning Centers, 2001.

Reeves, Doug. "Of Hubs, Bridges, and Networks." *Educational Leadership* 63, no. 8 (June 2006): 32–37.

Sanders, William, and Joan Rivers. "Cumulative and Residual Effects of Teachers on Future Student Academic Achievement." University of Tennessee Value-Added Research and Assessment Center, Knoxville. November 1996.

Sarason, S. *The Predictable Failure of Educational Reform: Can We Change Course Before It's Too Late?* San Francisco: Jossey-Bass, 1990.

Scherer, Marge. "The Challenge to Change." *Educational Leadership* 63, no. 8 (May 2006).

Sitting Bull. Available at http://en.thinkexist.com/quotes/sitting_bull

Sizer, Theodore R. *The Red Pencil*. New Haven: Yale University Press, 2004.

Sizer, Theodore R, and Nancy Faust-Sizer. *The Students Are Watching: Schools and the Moral Contract*. Boston: Beacon Press, 1999.

Somerville, Janice I. "Activity." *ACT* 42, no. 1 (Winter 2004): 1, 10.

"Succeeding Together at the Met." Available at http://www.whatkidscando.org/portfoliosmallschools/MET/Metintro.html

"Sweeping Revamp for DPS." *Denver Post, The* (9 December 2004): sec 1A and 15A.

Terkel, Studs. *Working.* New York: New York Press, 1972, 1974.

Tu, Chih-Hsiung, and Michael Corry. "Introduction." *Research in Online Learning Community*, 2002. Available at http.//www.usq.edu.au/electpub/e-jist/docs/html2002/chtu.html

Vander Ark, Tom. Keynote speech at CASE High School Summit, Copper Mountain, Colorado, 10 June 2004.

Volmer, Jamie. A speech given to Littleton Public Schools' administrators in Littleton, Colorado, 3 August 2004.

Webb, L. Dean and Roger Berkbuegler. *Personal Learning Plans for Educators.* Reston, VA: The National Association of Secondary School Principals, 1998.

Wiggins, Grant, and Jay McTighe. "Examining the Teaching Life," *Educational Leadership* 63, no. 6 (March 2006): 26–29.

Wurtzel, Judy. *Transforming High School Teaching and Learning: A District-wide Design.* Washington, D.C.: The Aspen Institute, 2006.

Zmuda, Allison, Robert Kuklis, and Everett Kline. *Transforming Schools: Creating a Culture of Continuous Improvement.* Alexandria, VA: ASCD, 2004.